About the Author

Stephen Sturgess has been practising yoga and meditation since 1969, when he was first introduced to it by Swami Pragyamurti, a direct disciple of Paramhansa Satyananda Saraswati of the Bihar School of Yoga in India.

During those 48 years, Stephen has studied, practised and experienced the different paths of yoga and meditation – *hatha, raja, kriya, kundalini, tantra, jnana, karma* and *bhakti* – which increased his spiritual insights, experience and spiritual knowledge. While following these different paths, he studied under well-known yoga masters. These include three of Swami Sivananda Saraswati's (of Rishikesh) foremost disciples: Swami Satyananda Saraswati, Swami Venkatesananda and Swami Vishnudevananda. These inspiring Yoga gurus were making regular visits to London in the 1970s.

Stephen was initiated by Swami Satyananda Saraswati in 1979 and given the spiritual name of Shankara. It was also in this year that he received the 'British Wheel of Yoga Teaching Diploma' and began teaching Yoga.

Stephen also met and studied Yoga and *prāṇāyāma* during the 1970s under the expertise of Yoga Maharishi Dr Swami Gitananda of Pondicherry, India.

In 1982, Stephen met Swami Kriyananda (a direct disciple of Paramhansa Yogananda, author of *Autobiography of a Yogi*) in London. The night after meeting Swami Kriyananda, Paramhansa Yogananda appeared to Stephen in a superconscious dream and told him that he was his guru, and that the Kriya Yoga path is the path he should follow. Then, in 1983, Swami Kriyananda personally initiated him into the ancient science of Kriya that Mahavatar Babaji taught to Lahiri Mahasaya, and that was passed down in succession to Swami Sri Yukteswar, and then, Paramhansa Yogananda.

For 26 years, Stephen led the Ananda Kriya Meditation Group in London. Then, in 2011, Stephen was ordained as a Kriya Yoga Meditation Teacher (*Kriyācharya*) to teach and initiate others into Kriya meditation by Roy Eugene Davis (1931–2019), a direct disciple of Paramhansa Yogananda, who was the director of the Centre for Spiritual Awareness (Georgia, USA).

In addition to his primary devotion to Yoga and meditation, and related subjects, Stephen has a BA (Hons) Ayurveda Degree from Thames Valley University (2004). He is also a graphic designer, artist and a writer. He lives in London and continues to guide and inspire others on the spiritual path of Kriya Yoga Meditation.

Stephen is also the author of *The Yoga Book*, *The Book of Chakras and the Subtle Bodies*, *Yoga Meditation* (published by Watkins Publishing, London),

The Supreme Art and Science of Raja and Kriya Yoga (Singing Dragon Publishers) and *Mastering the Mind, Realising the Self* (O-Books).

Stephen teaches Kriya Yoga Meditation in London and initiates those who have spiritually prepared and are ready for commitment to practising Kriya meditation.

Stephen can be reached at:

Website: www.yogananda-kriyayoga.org.uk

Dedication

I dedicate this book with love and gratitude to my
beloved spiritual guru, Paramhansa Yogananda
(1893–1952), the embodiment of grace, wisdom and
love, who appeared to me in a superconscious dream
in 1982, and his direct disciple Swami Kriyananda
(1926–2013), who wisely taught and guided me for
30 years on the Kriya Yoga path of meditation.

Stephen Sturgess

WILLPOWER AND ENERGY

YOGANANDA'S ENERGISATION EXERCISES

AUSTIN MACAULEY PUBLISHERS™

LONDON * CAMBRIDGE * NEW YORK * SHARJAH

A CIP catalogue record for this title is available from the British Library.

ISBN 9781788789240 (Paperback)
ISBN 9781528956390 (ePub e-book)

www.austinmacauley.com

First Published (2019)
Austin Macauley Publishers Ltd
25 Canada Square
Canary Wharf
London
E14 5LQ

Acknowledgements

I am very grateful to Violaine le Delezir for modelling for *Yogananda's Energisation Exercises*, and to Katerina Kyrou for modelling for *Swami Kriyananda's Superconscious Living Exercises*, and for Laura Archini who modelled for the *Aum Technique*.

I am also grateful to all those who took the time to write their testimonials for their experience of practising Yogananda's Energisation Exercises. A big, warm 'thank you' to you all!

Preface

As I write this book, I am reminded that this year, 2016, is the 100th anniversary of Paramhansa Yogananda's innovation of the principle of life force control (*pranayama*) that he devised and developed in his system of *Energisation Exercises*, in India, 1916. In the beginning, Yogananda used the term *Yogoda* as the name of his teachings and his spiritual organisation in India (Yogoda Satsanga Society); this included the *Energisation Exercises* (Yogoda Exercises). The word *Yogoda* is derived from the Sanskrit word *Yoga* meaning union; and *da* meaning 'that which imparts'. *Yogoda* means a system of Yoga that imparts harmony, equilibrium and unity to the mind, body and soul. *Sat* means 'truth', and *Sanga* means 'community' or 'assembly'.

In his *Autobiography of a Yogi* (original edition, 1946), Paramhansa Yogananda wrote:

> "The ideal of an all-sided education for youth had always been close to my heart; I saw clearly the arid results of ordinary instruction, aimed only at the development of body and intellect. Moral and spiritual values, without whose appreciation no man can approach happiness, were yet lacking in the formal curriculum. I determined to found a school where young boys could develop to the full stature of manhood. My first step in that direction was made with seven children at Dhikia, a small country site in Bengal.
>
> "A year later, in 1918, through the generosity of Sir Mahindra Chandra Nundy, the Maharaja of Kasimbazar, I was able to transfer my fast-growing group to Ranchi. This town in Bihar, about two hundred miles from Calcutta, is blessed with one of the healthiest climates in India. The Kasimbazar Palace at Ranchi was transformed into the headquarters for the new school, which I called *Brahmacharya Vidyalaya* in accordance with the educational ideals of the rishis. Their forest ashrams had been the ancient seats of learning, secular and divine, for the youth of India.
>
> "At Ranchi, I organised an educational programme for both grammar and high school grades. It included agricultural, industrial, commercial and academic subjects. The students were also taught yoga concentration and meditation, and a unique system of physical development, *Yogoda*, whose principles I had discovered in 1916.
>
> "Realising that man's body is like an electric battery, I reasoned that it could be recharged with energy through the direct agency of the

human will. As no action, slight or large, is possible without *willing*, man can avail himself of his prime mover, will, to renew his bodily tissues without burdensome apparatus or mechanical exercises. I therefore taught the Ranchi students my simple *Yogoda* techniques by which the life force, centred in man's medulla oblongata, can be consciously and instantly recharged from the unlimited supply of cosmic energy."

Paramhansa Yogananda's Energisation Exercises

In his book *'Paramhansa Yogananda As I Knew Him'*, Roy Eugene Davis (a direct disciple of Paramhansa Yogananda) says:

"Master innovated 'Energisation Exercises' before he came to America. He read about exercise routines used by Friedrich Wilhelm Muller, a German man born in Prussia who, in the early years of the 1900s, gave public demonstrations of strength and muscle control using the name Eugen Sandow. He taught that tensing and relaxing his muscles might produce benefits similar to be had by actually exercising.

"Master's idea was, that mild tension of muscles while visualising and willing energy to flow from the medulla oblongata at the base of the brain to the muscles, might improve muscle strength while vitalising the body.

"Energy is drawn from that brain region when tensing and allowed to return when relaxing because some yogis say that it is where soul force comes into the physical body."

The basic Recharging Exercises (Energization Exercises) come directly from a book by the famous strong man Eugen Sandow. Yogananda found a copy of his book in India before coming to America. He was with Swami Satyananda Giri at the time, and as he picked up the book he said, "There is something in here for us." However, Yogananda greatly innovated and elaborated on the exercises.

Yogananda probably drew his inspiration and innovation for using positive thinking with affirmations in his teachings from his association with the New Thought Movement that begun in the 1800s, and that emphasised holistic living, optimistic thinking, healing, prayer and meditative contemplation. Yogananda spoke at an International New Thought Alliance Conference in New York City in 1926 and had friendships with many New Thought teachers.

Yogananda's work extended far beyond SRF (Self-Realization Fellowship). He was best friends with H. Spencer Lewis, the founder of the Rosicrucian Order (AMORC), and had great influence on Lewis' teachings. Also, Yogananda was the creator of Science of Mind (Church of Religious Science) through his student Ernest Holmes. As a young man, Holmes visited Yogananda and asked to learn from him. "Yoga is not your path," Yogananda told him, "your way is through the mind. Come here once a week and I will teach you." So, for some years, Holmes learned from him and then, at Yogananda's direction, wrote the book *Science of Mind* and started the church. Between the years 1961-62, at least one third of the members at the SRF Hollywood Church had come to SRF through Science of Mind studies.

The *Energisation Exercises* (previously known as '*Tissue –Will System of Body and Mind Perfection*') were developed by Paramhansa Yogananda initially as a means by which the boys at his school in Ranchi, India, could focus their youthful energies in a positive way and develop their will power. The *Energisation Exercises* consists of thirty-nine psychophysical exercises that combine various physical movements with alternate tension and relaxation of the muscles, with breathing techniques and using concentrated attention to draw abundant energy consciously into the body by *will power*.

The *Energisation Exercises* can be used to develop your will power, by using concentrated attention to draw abundant energy consciously into your body at all times from the eternal limitless Source of Cosmic Energy that is within and around you, recharging it with energy and vitality. With such will power and life energy, you can experience your spiritual, subtle nature and positively transform your life.

The *Energisation Exercises* are to be practised twice a day every day. The 39 exercises are practised in a specific order and their practice takes between 12 to 15 minutes. The simplicity of these exercises is that they can all be practised from a standing position in a very small space. You do not need to use a Yoga mat or even wear Yoga clothes. These exercises are like a portable exercise system that you can take anywhere with you and practise in small spaces. All you need to do is memorise the exact sequence in which they are to be practised and then practise them correctly. The quickest and clearest way to practise them is to find a teacher who can demonstrate how they are practised.

These techniques systematically purify and strengthen all the body parts with vital force (*prāna*), giving health, strength and vitality to the body. The memory and brainpower are also increased, giving clarity and harmony to the mind. The *Energisation Exercises* invigorate the mind with vitality and enthusiasm, creating a spiritually elevating influence on one's attitude to daily life.

The physical benefits of these exercises are important for keeping your body fit and healthy, but their primary benefit is that their practice strengthens the *will power*, which is the cornerstone of the science of Raja Yoga and an essential tool for the practice of *Kriya*.

Yogananda said, "*Will power is what makes you divine. When you give up using that will, you become a mortal man... If you continuously use your will power, no matter what reverses come, it will produce success and health and power to help people, and above all, it will produce communion with God.*"

The *Energisation Exercises* are a wonderful addition to *Kriya Yoga* – the universal science of God-realisation that is spiritually transforming millions of lives throughout the world.

The Masters of Kriya Yoga

The ancient science of Kriya Yoga, which had been lost and forgotten for many centuries made its reappearance in the world when in 1861, Shyama Charan Lahiri (now more respectively known as Lahiri Mahasaya) – a young Bengali head clerk who was working in a region of the foothills of the Himalayas – met his immortal guru, Mahavatar Babaji, near Ranikhet, and received initiation from him into the ancient science of Kriya Yoga meditation. Although he was a married householder and not a renunciant, he was given special permission by Babaji to teach Kriya meditation, not only to renounced yogis, but also to those sincere devotees who were married with family and worldly responsibilities like himself. Babaji told Lahiri Mahasaya, "The Kriya Yoga that I am giving to the world through you in this nineteenth century is a revival of the same science that Krishna gave millenniums ago to Arjuna and that was later known to Patanjali and Christ, and to St John, St Paul and other disciples."

Over the next three decades, Lahiri Mahasaya lived as an ideal householder in the holy city of Banaras by the river Ganges (now known as Varanasi), where he initiated several thousand devotees in *Kriya Yoga*.

In 1894, one of Lahiri Mahasaya's leading disciples, Swami Sri Yukteswar, who had been initiated by Lahiri Mahasaya in 1883, met Babaji at a *Kumbha Mela* (a spiritual fair) in Allahabad, held on the banks of the River Ganges, attended by thousands of yogis and spiritual seekers. At that time, Babaji told Swami Sri Yukteswar, "You, swamiji, have a part to play in the coming harmonious interchange between Orient and Occident. Some years, hence, I shall send you a disciple whom you can train for Yoga dissemination in the West. The vibrations there of many spiritually seeking souls come floodlike to me. I perceive potential saints in America and Europe, waiting to be awakened."

Yogananda was blessed to have parents that were both disciples of Lahiri Mahasaya. When Yogananda (known as Mukundalal) was a baby, his parents took him to receive blessings from Lahiri Mahasaya, who predicted the future of Mukundalal saying, "This baby, when he grows up, will enlighten the whole universe with his divine wisdom and will guide many spiritual aspirants on the path of Kriya Yoga."

As a child, Mukundalal received initiation into the *Kriya* technique of meditation, and later, when he was seventeen, he met his divine Guru, Swami Sri Yukteswar, and received the *Kriya* initiation with spiritual blessings from him. In 1915, Swami Sri Yukteswar formally initiated Mukundalal into the renunciant Swami Order (*Sannyas*) as a monk and named him Swami Yogananda Giri. Later, he was bestowed with the highest spiritual title, Paramhansa Yogananda.

Later, in 1920, Babaji personally told Yogananda: "You are the one I have chosen to spread the message of Kriyā Yoga in the West. Long ago, I met your guru Yukteswar at a Kumbha Mela; I told him then I would send you to him for training."

And so, it was as predicted. Yogananda was sent by his guru from India to disseminate the teachings of Kriya Yoga worldwide. He travelled to America to attend a seminar of world religions in Boston organised by the Congress of Religious Liberals as a representative of India. After his successful talk, thousands of Americans took *Kriya Initiation* from him and were blessed by him.

> *"Kriya Yoga, the scientific technique of God-realisation,*
> *will ultimately spread in all lands, and aid in harmonising*
> *the nations through man's personal, transcendental*
> *perception of the Infinite Father."*
> Paramhansa Yogananda (*Autobiography of a Yogi*, 1946)

Paramhansa Yogananda lived and taught the spiritual teachings of Kriya Yoga in America for 30 years, where he established the organisation in Los Angeles, California, called Self-Realisation Fellowship (SRF). He left his body in superconscious communion with God, known as *Mahasamadhi*, in March 1952.

Yogananda is known worldwide by his spiritually inspiring classic book, *Autobiography of a Yogi*. The original edition was published in 1946.

The Ancient Science of Kriya Yoga

"Kriyā, controlling the mind directly through the
life force, is the easiest, most effective and most
scientific avenue of approach to the Infinite."
Paramhansa Yogananda (Autobiography of a Yogi, 1946)

Kriyā Yoga is the essence and synthesis of all Yogas and religions, which includes the ancient and highest yoga and meditation techniques from Haṭha Yoga, Raja Yoga, Laya Yoga and Mantra Yoga.

The Sanskrit word Kriyā means 'to do', 'action', and Yoga means 'union'. Kriyā Yoga therefore means a certain action or active process to achieve the science of uniting the individual self with the Supreme Self. Kriyā is a specific meditation technique which leads to Self- and God-realisation. Traditionally, this Kriyā technique can be revealed only to initiates.

This ancient spiritual art and science of Kriyā Yoga awakens the divine memory of the Self, of which it has forgotten its real nature due to identification and attachment to the body, mind and ego-self.

We have forgotten that our soul or inner Self and God, the Ultimate Reality are One, so we must learn to manifest our Divinity by letting go of false ideas about self-identity, and by weakening and removing conditions which interfere with or prevent spiritual awakening. When we realise this, then we will discover that we are Divine, everything is God, and nothing exists but God.

Kriyā Yoga is the quickest means of attaining spiritual success. By practising Kriyā Yoga, a person transcends human consciousness and attains Divine Consciousness.

It is through the divine dispensation, through a great line of Spiritual Masters: Christ, Krishna, Mahavatar Babaji, Lahiri Mahasaya and Swami Sri Yukteswar, that Paramhansa Yogananda was selected and blessed to impart the supreme science of Kriyā Yoga worldwide.

Kriya Initiation and the Blessings of the Guru

When Babaji gave Lahiri Mahasaya permission to initiate others into *Kriyā Yoga,* he also told him to advise each new initiate in the words of Krishna (*Bhāgavad Gīta*, 2:40): *"Even a little of the practice of this dharma will save you from great fear."*

Kriya Yoga, practised with the divine blessings of the Guru bestowed at the time of the sacred *Kriya Initiation*, reverses the outward flowing life force in the body and raises the consciousness and life force inward and upward through the astral centres of consciousness (*chakras*) in the astral spine, through the same pathway by which it had descended into the body and senses, to be reunited again in the infinite state of *divine Awareness.*

Three Powerful Kriya Techniques

This book I have written is a practical companion guide to Yogananda's *Autobiography of a Yogi.* It covers three of Yogananda's practical and powerful detailed techniques of Kriya Yoga: *The Energisation Exercises, Hong-Sau Technique* and *the Aum Technique* (For the complete Kriya preparation techniques and teachings of *Kriya Yoga*, I suggest you read my books: *The Art and Science of Raja & Kriya Yoga* and *Yoga Meditation*). These three basic techniques, that bring spiritual and practical benefits, can be learned and practised by anyone, of any faith, on any path. If you practise these techniques regularly on a daily basis with dedication and devotion, you will be able to interiorise your mind, and absorb it into the thought of the divine Self within you. The *Energisation Exercises* will give you the will power, willingness, enthusiasm and energy to meditate, and will enhance your meditation; the *Hong-Sau* technique will calm your mind and deepen your concentration; and the *Aum* technique will take you deeper into meditation. By listening inwardly beyond the gross vibrations of the outer world, to the inner awareness of the subtle sounds of the *chakras* and to the blissful sound of *Aum*, the 'Word of God' – the Cosmic Vibration, that sustains every particle of creation in the Cosmos – you will experience the love, wisdom, bliss and peace of God, the supreme Self within you.

These three techniques will keep your enthusiasm alive with ever-new joy and will prepare you for the ancient *Kriya Meditation* technique that Paramhansa Yogananda initiated disciples into. This technique is not given in this book as one has to prepare for it physically, mentally and spiritually. One can apply for *Kriya Initiation* to a recognised teacher of Kriya who is authorised to initiate. But first, you must prepare for it by regularly practising the Kriya preparation techniques for a few months. You will need to be self-disciplined and regular in your daily practices, and you will also need to have the right attitudes and values, and to cultivate love and devotion towards God and the Kriya line of Gurus. Then, very importantly, it has to *feel* right in your own heart if you are going to make a commitment to the spiritual path of Kriya.

Regular daily practice of meditation will transform you from within. It will help you to perform all your worldly duties and attend to your responsibilities serenely, saturated with inner calmness and peace. Remember, true happiness and lasting fulfilment is not found outwardly in the world of the senses and restless desires, but in the silent depths of your being, the inner changeless Self.

You have *free will* to choose. You have the *will power* to choose where you focus your attention. If your consciousness is predominantly with the world, then you are ruled by the *dualities* of the world. If your attention is focused inwardly, to reawakening your divine awareness of *oneness* with God, the supreme Self, then you can rise above ignorance and suffering, overcome self-defeating habits of thought and behaviour, and live your life in a way that joyously affirms your divine birth right of love, wisdom and freedom.

Spiritually awakening to realisation of your pure essential nature (the indwelling Self) and knowledge of ultimate Reality, God, should be your highest aim in life, for the whole of the universe and human life is constructed on the reality of God. You hold *within* yourself that which you are seeking. The primary cause of lack of Self-awareness is a mistaken perception of self-identity.

The deep-rooted restlessness and a feeling that something is 'missing' that you experience in life, comes from the experience of *separation* from the love, peace and supreme bliss of God.

Meditation brings an end to separation and *unites* you with that supreme bliss of the inner God-Self. Regular daily practice of meditation will purify and strengthen your mind and bring clarity to it. Once you recognise the true meaning and value of the power of meditation, then you will meditate naturally with love and joy. You will have that *direct* experience of love and bliss from your inner divine Source. In that meditative silence of the senses, the presence of God will stand before you.

This book gives you the inspiration and tools to transform your mind and realise your true essential blissful nature; to experience the presence of the changeless God-Self *within* you. Whether you believe in God or not, you cannot deny that you have a basic desire for *happiness*. No one in their right mind desires unhappiness, suffering and sorrow. We all want freedom in joy! Not the short-lived joys that we get from sensual pleasures, attachments, frustrated desires, fame and praise, but the ever-lasting and perfect joy that is non-dependent and is free from likes and dislikes. A true joy and real happiness that is the very nature of your own inner Self and is the essence of every living being.

Testimonials from Those Practising Yogananda's Energisation Exercises

The following testimonials are given by devotees of Paramhansa Yogananda, who have been practising Kriya Yoga and the *Energisation Exercises* on a daily basis for some years, or in some cases for many years.

How often do you practise them?

Twice a day without fail just before morning and evening meditations (sometimes a third time if I feel I need an 'energy boost' in the middle of the day).

Do you feel the energy immediately after practising them?

Absolutely, and all throughout the day.

How does it affect your meditation?

Meditation is always very much deeper when I energise first – the difference is like night and day. Easy to feel the difference!

How do the Energisation Exercises affect your everyday living and work?

I have much, much more energy for everything I want and need to do in daily life.

Does the energy sustain you throughout the day?

Yes!

Have they improved your will power and willingness?

Absolutely! Master makes a lot of amazing statements and promises about their effectiveness, and I have proved to myself that everything he says about them is true and more!

Has your health (physical/mental) improved through practising the *Energisation Exercises*?

I have been doing these exercises faithfully for over 40 years. I cannot say enough good things about them. I know, without question, that my health is much better (mental and physical) than it would have been if I had not been doing them all these years.

Any other thoughts on these wonderful exercises?

They are indeed amazing and wonderful! Several years after I first received initiation into Kriya Yoga, I was having trouble with my meditations. One day, as I was praying for help with my difficulties, I heard an answer quite clearly: "You should practice the *Energisation Exercises* with more determination, energy and will power!" From that point onward, I said to myself, "I may never be the world's greatest meditator, but I KNOW I can become a 'World Champion Energiser'!" So from that point onward, I began to Energie with greater and greater 'willingness power' and with all my heart. And, it worked! My meditations became stronger, longer and much deeper almost immediately. I now consider myself to be a 'World Champion Energiser'. (Smile) Onward and upward!

Nayaswami Savitri – author, Ananda Sangha worldwide minister/teacher, spiritual counsellor, and devoted *Kriyaban*. For more information please visit www.savitrisimpson.com

"These sacred exercises are unique, in the actual movements and breathing techniques as well as the philosophy behind them. I find over the years that they allow me to experience my physical body as a temple bathed in divine energy. Practicing the *Energisation Exercises* helps me to remember that I am a soul living in a body and not merely a body living in this world. They bring a grace to the human form that allows our soul nature, in all its brilliance, to shine through."

Lila Devi – founder of Spirit-in-Nature Essences (established 1977) and author, including *From Bagels to Curry*.

"I practice Yogananda's *Energisation Exercises* before meditation. I meditate twice a day. I love them because they channel and focus my energy and attention, which is exactly what I want to be doing in meditation anyway. So, they're very efficient; they get me there quicker than not doing them!

"They are like meditation, in that I just can't imagine *not* doing them – I feel so much better when I do!

"Health (physical/mental) – I have been practicing the *Energisation Exercises* and meditation for 30 years, and I am very blessed, in that I just can't recall any (or at most, only one or two) times I've had any significant health challenge. Nothing but positives. Thank you, Yogananda!"

Dambara Begley – Ananda Minister and Teacher.

"I have been practicing Yogananda's *Energisation Exercises* daily for almost 30 years. They are part of my regular sadhana, keeping me healthy and preparing me for meditation. I definitely feel their energetic effect. The best part of them is that they can be taken to ever-deeper levels. For example, one learns not only to *feel* and *send* prana, but to *withdraw* it, which is a key for spiritual unfoldment. I apply their principles also to my Kriya Yoga practice, and to Ananda Yoga. They are, for me, at the heart of Yogananda's teaching."

Jayadev Jaerschky – Director of the Ananda Yoga School of Europe.

"It has been my great blessing to have learnt and practised, almost daily, for over thirty years now, the *Energisation Exercises* taught by Yogananda. This daily routine is excellent for keeping my body and mind, full of vitality and *prana*. Interestingly, if for any reason I have been unable to practise the routine, I usually feel more sluggish and dull throughout the day. With regular practise, I have noticed that you become more and more identified with the *pranic* electricity contained within the body and of the power of your mind and will power to consciously direct that energy, to keep your muscles and body strong. As someone with a chronic medical condition, taking daily medication, I cannot but give thanks for the great blessings of these exercises in my life.

Another story which comes to mind, is a question that a student put to Yogananda about the *Hong-Sau* technique. The student asked Master what tips he would give to help deepen their practise of the *Hong-Sau* technique. Yogananda replied: "Practise the *Energisation Exercises* with deep concentration. This is the greatest way to help you go deep in meditation."

Tony Sananda O'Connell

"I attribute my constant, high level of energy and robust health to three factors: my Guru's grace, the practice of Kriya and to the *Energisation Exercises*. The Ananda Life Therapy School for Self-Healing is based primarily on these exercises, and students all over the world are discovering that they are the very essence of healing, bringing pranic life force to every cell of the body."

Nayaswami Shivani – co-founder Yogananda Academy of Europe.

"I rarely miss a day without doing the *Energisation Exercises.* Yogananda had said if you were stranded on a desert island and only had the time for practicing one technique, that would be the one. It is that essential and helpful. Those practising it know how it gets blood flow to the whole body to energise it and prepare it for meditation. It helps in focusing and clearing the mind for meditation and releases stress. There is a power in practicing them, in tuning into the great energy of Paramhansa Yogananda. There's a long list of benefits. The one many people do not know that was instrumental to my healing from an autoimmune disorder when doctors did not say it was possible, is that it teaches voluntary action of muscles that would normally operate involuntarily. Thus, it trains you to have even more control over your whole body and internal organs directing them towards your desired healing."

Avital Miller – international keynote speaker and author of *Healing Happens: Stories of Healing against All Odds*."
www.healinghappensbook.com, www.avitalmiller.com

"For the first few years that I practiced the *Energisation Exercises,* I did them faithfully but, as is unfortunately often the case, without a deep understanding of what they were really about. Some years ago, I found myself in a situation where I had to teach the *Energisation Exercises.* In order to prepare, I started to study Yogananda's words on energisation, watch videos of Kriyananda doing the exercises, and receive personal instruction from experienced teachers. My practice transformed in about a week! One of the immediate benefits was a remarkable increase in my focus and concentration in meditation. Up until that point, I had been drinking a tiny amount of coffee or green tea before meditations to help me to keep my mind awake and sharp (not enough to agitate the mind, as happens when one drinks coffee in larger quantities). I found that my deeper practice of energisation gave me so much focus that I was able to do away with these 'aids' completely and have never used them since. This period was also incredibly intense: a month of long and active days with hardly any time off, or sleep. The *Energisation Exercises* helped me to make it through this period. Every morning, before getting out of bed, I would do the 20 body parts several times. Without this little ritual, it was difficult to get out of bed.

"I continue to practice the *Energisation Exercises* faithfully and regularly, but now I practice them with reverence, joy and a desire to experience their secrets ever more deeply. Thank you Yogananda, for this gift to mankind!"

Mahiya Matthews, resident of *Ananda Europa*, author of *A Taste of Joy.*

"I have now been practicing Yogananda's *Energisation Exercises* for about 16 years. They are very special to me. This form of exercises is very unique, it prepares the body for meditation and it allows the Kriya Yoga practice to be much more profound and powerful.

"What I like of these exercises is that I can take them with me wherever I go, they don't require any props or equipment in order to be practised but just a sincere soul, and even if there is hardly any space around me, if I can stand then I can practise.

"In my daily practice, I practise them before my yoga asanas followed by meditation, I believe that they energise my body, refresh my mind and nourish my soul."

Giulia Tripepi, Kriya initiate devotee of Yogananda, London, UK.

"I started practising the *Energisation Exercises* four years ago, and I still do it every morning.

"On a physical point of view, the energy released immediately after practising them makes me feel well and strong all day, and sometimes I realise it's lunch time, but I don't feel the need of eating. Since I've been practising them, my health has improved, and I rarely get ill. On a spiritual point of view, the heat I feel in my spine and at the point of the medulla oblongata (in the brain stem at the back of the head) is a sign they are working on a more subtle level and I easily go into a deep meditation.

"They are very easy to practice, because they were specifically created to be accessible for everyone. Paramahansa Yogananda started them in 1917 with the children of the school in Ranchi in India and, as he would say, they are the scientific application of yoga principles in the everyday life, showing that *prana* energy is immediately accessible and can nurture and heal the body, improve the brain functions and affect our subtle levels.

"They will help you to release stress and anxieties, feeling connected, positive, whole and well."

Laura Archini, Kriya initiate devotee of Yogananda, London, UK.

"The primary effect I've experienced from the *Energisation Exercises* is the simple but profound understanding of what 'relaxation' really feels like. In so much of life we learn to tense, but seldom learn to relax. The *Energisation Exercises* teach how tension and relaxation are two sides of the same coin, and that just as tensing can be done consciously, so can relaxation. Thus, when someone says, "Just relax," you actually know how to do it! (This is so important that it's one of the central themes in my book from Crystal Clarity Publishers called 'Solving Stress'). By the practice of *Energisation Exercises*, I've become much more deeply aware of when my body is experiencing tension and have developed the ability to then let that tension go. As a result, I seldom carry any physical tension in my body, which has had significant repercussions on health and happiness. The energy that's so often trapped in tense muscles is readily available to focus on any number of other tasks, including my work, play, time with family, and every other part of life. In short, they are one of the greatest gifts of Yogananda's teachings."

Satyaki, resident at Ananda Village, Nevada City, California.

"I have been practicing *Energisation Exercises* since I joined Ananda in 1969. They have been my companion through all the ups and downs of life, spiritual and otherwise. I was single when I joined Ananda, then married after four years. The birth of our daughter disrupted our schedules, of course, but after some time my husband, Jaya, and I made a New Year's resolution to begin practicing again at least once a day. Yes, there have been periods when one or both of us missed quite a few sessions, but the power of the *Energisation Exercises* keeps bringing us back.

"Now in my 70s, I have arthritis in my spine, and the *Energisation Exercises* are the thing that gets me up and going again. I usually have a lot of stiffness and much pain in the morning but practicing the exercises (gently at first) helps this to improve quite a bit. Sometimes, I have to hold onto the kitchen counter or the back of a chair to minimise stress on my back, and I sometimes can only do about half of the exercises at one time. However, after a very short break of five minutes or less I can return and finish."

Nayaswami Sadhana Devi, resident at Ananda Village, Nevada City, California.

"I was first introduced to the Energisation Exercises through the Self-Realization Fellowship back in the early 1980s. In the beginning, it took me some time to learn and memorise the sequence of the 39 exercises as I didn't have a teacher to teach me in person. I only had the SRF lessons on printed paper to look at with matchstick drawings of the exercises. Then, I visited Ananda Europa on a Kriya Yoga retreat in Assisi, Italy, and learnt them quickly by practising them twice a day everyday guided by a teacher. I'm very self-disciplined, and so I have continued my practice since the 1980s. I always start my day everyday with the Energization Exercises. They give me abundant energy which lasts all day. I take that energy into my Kriya meditation, up through the spine to the higher brain centres. Then I practice my Kriya breath meditation and finish by sitting in silent stillness for some time. I have also had success in using the Energisation Exercises to heal a back and a knee problem by using my willpower and sending the energy direct to heal the physical ailments."

Stephen Sturgess, Kriya Meditation teacher, London, UK.

Consciousness and Cosmic Energy

*"The conscious cosmic energy first enters through
the medulla oblongata (in the brain stem) and
remains concentrated in the brain as the
thousand-petalled lotus. Then it descends
into the body through the spinal cord
and sympathetic nervous system."*
Paramhansa Yogananda.

Science and Energy

Christiaan Huygens (1629–1695), the Dutch mathematician, astronomer and physicist, founded the wave theory of light. In his *Treatise on Light,* he argued a revised version of Descartes views, in which the speed of light is infinite and propagated by means of spherical waves emitted along the wave front. Huygens also discovered the true shape of the rings of the planet Saturn and made original contributions to the science of dynamics – the study of the action of forces on bodies.

Energy is a concept that took 178 years after Isaac Newton (1643–1727), to develop. Newton, an English scientist, was one of the most influential scientists of all time, who put forward numerous theories and contributed ideas to many different fields including physics, mathematics and philosophy. Newton's three laws of motion relate the forces acting on a body to its motion. The first is the law of inertia, it states that 'every object in motion will stay in motion until acted upon by an outside force'. The second is commonly stated as 'force equals mass times acceleration', or $F=ma$. The third and final law is known as 'to every action there is an equal and opposite reaction'.

In 1905, Albert Einstein (1879–1955), a theoretical physicist, postulated the theory of special relativity, which is the well confirmed physical theory regarding the relationship between space and time, and the matter/energy relationship, or $E=mc^2$ as most of us know it. This suggested that tiny particles of matter could be converted into vast amounts of energy, foreshadowing the development of atomic power. His general theory of relativity was completed in 1915. The culmination of his research was fully recognised in 1919 during a solar eclipse, when observations and measurements by British astronomers Sir Frank Dyson and Sir Arthur Eddington affirmed Einstein's assertions regarding how gravitational forces worked in regard to planetary orbits around the sun. This observation overturned Isaac Newton's concept of the universe, stating that space, distance and motion were not absolute but relative.

All of Life Is Consciousness and Energy

All of life is Consciousness and Energy, which are two aspects of the same Ultimate Reality. Cosmic Consciousness and Cosmic Energy pervades the universe and is beyond the universe. This Consciousness and Energy is in all things visible or invisible, conceivable or inconceivable, animate or inanimate. It is in every tree, rock, grain of sand, blade of grass, drop of water, insect, fish, bird, animal and human; all is vibrating with timeless All-Pervasive Consciousness and Cosmic Energy. Every part of Consciousness holds within it the whole of creation.

> *"To see a World in a grain of sand,*
> *And Heaven in a Wild Flower,*
> *Hold Infinity in the palm of your hand,*
> *and Eternity in an hour."*
> **William Blake** (Auguries of Innocence)

Scientifically this can be understood according to Einstein's famous equation $E=mc2$, c being the speed of light (300,000 km per second, which is a universal constant of nature, absolute and not relative) and m for mass. This shows that mass and energy being mutually convertible, are intrinsically the same. There is no separation between matter and energy, or matter and mind. They are aspects of one energy. In other words, there is a basic oneness and unity of life. It is the Ultimate Reality that underlies and unifies the multiplicity of everything. This equation $E=mc2$ not only gives a clue to the production of energy which can be generated from a small amount of mass but its corollary gives an equation for mass that is $m=E/c2$; and that a beam of light is pure energy ($c-E/mc$). It gives also a clue to the power and potential of a human being.

The Difference Between the Path of Science and Spirituality

The path of science and spirituality are the same – they both seek truth or the key to unlocking the door to nature of Reality – *but the goals are different.* The goal of science is to reach a correct intellectual conception of the world and the universe. The scientist is guided by the mind and seeks only to know the world and the universe intellectually and does not seek anything more, whereas the spiritual seeker of Truth or the yogi is guided by the heart and wants to 'merge' with the Truth and not just intellectually know it.

Science has made tremendous achievements in medicine, and great leaps and bounds in technology, telecommunication, genetic engineering, biotechnology, cosmology and astrophysics (the study of gravitational waves and black holes) and quantum mechanics that gave us the foundation for nuclear physics and the physics of elementary particles (protons, neutrons, quarks, gluons) and condensed matter. Science has also taught us how to use logic and reason to understand the world and the universe that we live in. These great advances and achievements contributed by scientists cannot be denied, they must be acknowledged for the valuable contribution they have made in our lives. Yet, the most science can do is explore and map the surface of Reality and present us with a perceptual and conceptual view of the world and tell us that Consciousness is a product of the brain.

Even Einstein's $e=mc^2$, which demonstrated the inextricable relation of energy, matter and the speed of light, has not allowed physicist's to realise completely the reality of the universe. They are still searching for the 'beginning' of the universe, and posit that the beginning started with the 'Big Bang' theory – that the universe was created about 14 billion years ago as a small, dense and hot concentration of energy that exploded and creating in the process time, space and matter. The universe got differentiated into matter as the temperature of the universe cooled down, leading to the emergence of elementary particles of matter such as quarks and electrons, which further caused creation of stars, galaxies, planets, the beginning of life on Earth up to the birth of human beings.

The search for the smallest particle of matter still continues, quantum physics has reduced the fundamental fragment of the universe (the atom) first to electrons, positrons, and neutrons, then to neutrinos and antineutrinos, then further to photons, hadrons, quarks, antiquarks and mesons. Now quantum physics posit that even smaller particles can be discerned as waves, and an attempt to explain all of the particles and fundamental forces of nature in one theory is by modelling them as vibrations of tiny supersymmetric strings (*superstrings*).

The View of the Ancient Spiritual Sages

The ancient spiritual Sages of the East such as Lao Tzu, the Chinese Sage and legendary father of Taoism, who wrote the *Tao Te Ching* around the sixth century BCE, and the great Indian Sage Veda Vyasa, who wrote the *Mahabharata*, of which the *Bhagavad Gita* is a part of this great work, conclude that there was never a beginning of time, matter or space.

The *Bhagavad Gita* deals with such basic concepts as the nature of our existence, the nature of the true Self, our true relationship with God, the truth about action and non-action, the correct meaning of knowledge and ignorance, the meaning of true devotion, and the right attitude towards the external world.

According to the *Bhagavad Gita* the external world is unreal, not because it does not exist, but because it is unstable and ever-changing. Since it is based upon impermanence, it cannot be relied upon as a vehicle of truth, and it should not become the purpose of our existence. The teachings of the *Bhagavad Gita* show us a prominent reality that makes life more stable, peaceful and purposeful that is aligned to the central purpose of God's eternal Dharma, which is order and regularity. It discards untruth which surrounds us and reveals the changeless Self that exists in us all as the centre of truth and permanence, which we should ultimately discover.

According to Vedanta (one of the world's most ancient spiritual philosophies based on the *Vedas*, the sacred scriptures of India), the 'Big Bang Theory' is not the beginning of the universe; there have been infinite cycles of creation and dissolution of the universe. The entire universe was in an unmanifest condition before the current manifestation and will again become unmanifest.

The spiritual sciences of Yoga and Vedanta can teach the scientist that after knowing the world with the mind, further progress is still possible to unlock the door of the nature of Reality and to realise our own true nature as pure Consciousness. To do that we have to go beyond concepts and into the formlessness itself, to the *direct realisation* of oneself as that *Consciousness*.

> "Energy is within and around you,
> recharging the body at all times with vitality.
> You can call on that eternal supply
> to make the body fit in every respect."
> **Paramhansa Yogananda**.

Our Bodies Are Nothing but Energy

Ultimately, our bodies are nothing but energy. As Paramhansa Yogananda said, "Behind the light in every bulb is a great dynamic current; beneath every little wave is the vast ocean, which has become the wave." Our chakras act as dynamos of Cosmic Energy, allowing our subtle bodies to plug in to the universal power source. They serve as transformers and regulators to receive, assimilate and distribute *prāṇa* to the astral body, which then distributes it to the spinal nerve plexuses, where it is, in turn, transferred to the blood and organs of the physical body.

The *prāṇa* enters the body at the base of the brain in the brain stem, (an area known as the medulla oblongata. Yogananda referred to it as the 'mouth of God', the finite opening in the body through which God breathes His Cosmic Energy or Life into physical flesh) and flows to the higher brain centres. It then filters downward through the six major centres of consciousness (chakras) below that, starting at *ājñā chakra* (at the eyebrow centre) and working its way down to the base of the spine to *mūladhāra chakra*.

Sahasrāra (also known as *Brahmarandhra* 'the door of God') the main generator of the energies that power these six chakras, is located at the crown, above the medulla oblongata, and operates on a higher plane of consciousness.

As this energy spirals down through each chakra, it becomes increasingly dense, until it forms what are known as the 'five great elements' (*panchamahabhuta*). These are essential 'states' of matter, not to be confused with the periodic elements of modern chemistry, and they represent he stages of creation from Spirit to matter.

When these seven centres of consciousness and prāṇic energy are withdrawn from the body at death, the body disintegrates – the cosmic energy is switched off, and the soul has to leave the physical, astral and spiritual bodies through the seven astral doors or chakras in order to reach, and merge into the Spirit.

> "The spinal cord may be likened to a wire. In it are
> located these seven centres of light which are the
> sub-centres for the conduction and distribution
> of life current throughout the body. The body is
> nothing but a condensation of this spinal energy.
> Just as invisible hydrogen and oxygen atoms can
> be condensed into visible vapour, water and ice,
> so light can be transformed into body which is
> nothing but frozen energy."
> **Paramhansa Yogananda**.

Cosmic Energy projects the galaxies and governs the movement of the stars and planets. It is this same energy that is vibrating in our bodies and minds. We live, move and have our being in Consciousness that is whole, complete, self-contained and self-evolving. Consciousness is the field and the Source of all, and creation is the manifestation that happens from the Cosmic Energy within that.

Due to ignorance and the power of delusion, we have forgotten the Source of our being and the power of Supreme Consciousness and Cosmic Energy that permeates every particle of our being, and that is an inherent part of each of us. We are like a wave that gets separated from the ocean, it forgets it is a part of the ocean. Beneath the wave of your consciousness is the infinite ocean of Divine Consciousness – that potential of energy is so great within you that Yogananda said, "There is enough energy in a gram of flesh to run the city of Chicago for two days!"

Energy and Willpower

Energy is a manifestation of Consciousness, and Matter is a manifestation of that cosmic energy. This energy is available and accessible to us at all times, all we have to do is consciously plug into, or tune into it. Using the power of your will you can directly access and draw on the energy of the universe, which has an unlimited supply. My guru, Paramhansa Yogananda said, *"The stronger the will, the greater the flow of energy!"* The centre of positive will in the human body is the spiritual eye located at the eyebrow centre, the positive pole of the sixth centre of consciousness (*ājñā chakra*), and the seat of spiritual perception and intuition.

If you concentrate strongly with determination at that point between the eyebrows, you can draw on that limitless flow of Cosmic Energy through your medulla oblongata, the negative pole of the *ājñā chakra* and the seat of the ego, located in the brainstem at the base of the brain. Paramhansa Yogananda referred to the medulla oblongata as the 'mouth to God' and the 'doorway to God', meaning that it is the portal through which the body receives its energy from the universe and God.

"The astral body, in appearance like a vast nebula
or the tail of a comet, charges the physical body
with Cosmic Energy through the medulla oblongata."
Paramhansa Yogananda.

Feeling and Directing the Energy

Yogananda said that the medulla oblongata is fed by conscious Cosmic Energy which surrounds the body and which is drawn into the body by the *power of will*. Therefore, you should never say or think you are tired, for by doing so you become even more tired. Your will becomes paralysed with thoughts of tiredness and fatigue and cuts off the supply of energy. The will must be active in order to draw Cosmic Energy into the body.

We all have will power, but not all of us use it in a conscious way to draw energy into the body. Yogananda pointed out that many people die mentally long before they die physically: "When one ceases to have ambitions and to be interested in life, the will becomes paralysed. When this will-radio is untuned or destroyed, Cosmic Energy ceases to supply the reserve dynamo of the medulla, and physical health slowly fails from want of life force. This is the principle cause for the symptoms of old age. *The stronger the will, the greater the flow of energy into the tissues and body parts.*"

A simple test for you to feel and experience energy being directed by your will is to look at your right hand, palm upwards. First, let it relax, as it relaxes, the fingers naturally curl inward toward the palm. Now, stimulate an inward awareness of energy in your hand by slowly clenching your fist, and remembering what Yogananda said, *"The stronger the will, the greater the flow of energy into the tissues and body parts."* Using your concentrated willpower slowly tense your fist tighter and tighter, feeling the energy building up in the muscles of your fisted hand, until it is vibrating with energy (tension with *will* produces more energy than concentration alone). Then with awareness, slowly and gradually release the tension in the muscles of your hand to complete relaxation. Now relax and feel the energy. Compare the feeling in your right hand to the feeling in your left. You should notice a marked difference in energy.

These principles of energy to recharge the body at will were discovered and innovated by Paramhansa Yogananda in 1916, in India for his students, and were developed into the *Energisation Exercises*, a system of 39 exercises which teach one how to recharge the body with energy through the conscious power of will.

"The Energisation Exercises teach how to recharge
the body battery with fresh life current by increasing
the power of will. They strengthen and recharge the
muscles with vital force, not only collectively but
individually, and teach how to surround each body
cell with a ring of super-charged electrical vital-energy
and thus, keep them free from decay or bacterial invasion.
They keep not only the muscles, but also all the tissues of
the body, bones, marrow, brain and cells in perfect
health, and cause the resurrection of dying tissue cells
and worn out faculties, and the formation of
billions of new cells."
Paramhansa Yogananda.

Using 'Will and Energy' to Heal

When your energy level is high, it will be easier for you to feel and direct the energy flow toward the person you are praying for. Also, your willingness and empathy will be greater, allowing your concentration to stay focused and your heart open.

To be an effective channel for the Divine Will and to keep your energy level high, practise Yogananda's *Energisation Exercises* first, and then you will be able to act, pray and be divinely charged with greater energy!

The following technique of using energy for healing is a method that Paramhansa Yogananda taught.

1. Sit upright in a comfortable position. As you inhale deeply, slowly and gently tense all the muscles in your body. While tensing your body muscles, hold your breath in for a few seconds, and then exhale with a double breath (ha-haaa) through your mouth. Then relax and *feel* the energy flow into your body.

2. Now remain relaxed and calm. Touch your medulla oblongata at the base of the brain (the indentation at the back of the head, where the neck meets the skull) in order to make easier to concentrate on it. Then visualise Cosmic Energy surrounding and entering your body through the medulla and at the point between your eyebrows and flowing down into your spine.

3. Feel the energy flowing down the whole length of your arms into your hands. Continue tensing and relaxing your body and feeling the life force flow from the medulla and the point between your eyebrows through the spine to your hands.

4. Then stop tensing and relaxing, and by using your right palm, firmly rub your entire bare left arm up and down several times. Do the same to

your right arm with your left palm. Then relax, continuously visualising and willing Cosmic Energy to descend from the medulla through your arms into your hands.

5. Now, with closed eyes with your attention at the eyebrow centre, rapidly but gently rub your palms together about twenty times. Then separate your hands and raise them upward. You will feel the life current of energy flowing from the medulla into your spine, especially through both arms and hands, with a warm, tingling sensation.

Now that your hands are magnetised with energy, they can be used either for healing any diseased part of your own body or some other person's. If it is for another person, they need not be present, they can even be on the other side of the world. This Cosmic Energy or *prāṇic* energy passing through your hands has infinite power of projection. Energy follows thought. However, Yogananda said to visualise the person you are sending healing to. In other words, hold that person in God's healing Light, Love and Wholeness. Send that person healing on all three levels of their being – physical, mental and spiritual. And with unquestioning faith know that healing energy is working on all those levels, pouring strength, energy, power, love, light, and happiness into that person. Let there be no suggestion in your mind of limitation. Be like Jesus, who saw a person's wholeness, not their illness. See them with renewed life, vitality and strength. When you pray for others, do so affirmatively, seeing possibilities. If the person you are praying for has a health challenge, see that person radiantly well and revitalised. If the person you are praying for is seeking employment, then affirm divine guidance, fulfilment, abundance and new opportunities.

To send that healing force of energy through the ether or space after following the above steps, you can then raise your energy charged hands above your head with the palms facing forward. And with your eyes closed, and with your concentration at the eyebrow centre, send out through the palms of your hands divine currents of healing rays to the person who is unwell or diseased. As you do this, chant *Aum* aloud or mentally three times. Visualise and hold that person in the divine light for as long as you feel to do so.

It is best to prepare yourself for sending distant healing by meditating first until you are calm and still, then to offer a prayer to the Divine, so that you feel God's presence as the Divine Source of the healing you are sending.

You can use this prayer just before rubbing your hands together to magnetise and charge them with energy, then raising them to send the divine healing rays as you chant *Aum* three times: *"Divine Mother, Thou art omnipresent. Thy art in all Thy children. Thou art in (name of person you are sending healing to). Manifest Thy healing presence, love, peace, light and joy in his/her body."*

Sending Healing Prayers for World Peace

'Pray for one another, so that you may be healed.
The prayer of the righteous is powerful and effective.'
The Bible, James 5:16.

After praying for individual persons, you can send healing blessings out to the world to bring harmony and peace to all people.

Before praying for world peace, you may like to use the following prayer that I composed from the heart, to bring peace and harmony to yourself. Remember, a peaceful world begins with peaceful individuals. When peace, harmony and happiness has truly come to all individuals of every nation, then there will be world peace. For that to happen there has to be a positive change in consciousness. This is why the practice of daily meditation is important, because it brings inner calmness, inner peace and inner joy to the meditator. In a calm and focussed mind that is happy and at peace with itself there can be no room for stress, or such negative thoughts of hate and bad-will, and unfriendliness towards others. The practice of meditation is for the attainment of experiencing the perfection of the Self within. Once the embodied soul has seen the true nature of the Self, it becomes complete, fulfilled and free from sorrow. That divine inner Self is bliss, is love, is peace, and is harmony; that is its true divine essential nature, and it can be understood only after we attain that.

Heavenly Father grant me the wisdom to discriminate
wisely. Strengthen my will power to conquer and defeat
all wrong tendencies and bad habits in me. May your
Divine Light reveal the errors in my consciousness and
dissolve them completely. Lead me from darkness of
ignorance to Light of your Supreme Consciousness in
Truth and Eternal Joy. With your Divine blessings make
me a channel for love, peace and harmony.
Aum, Peace, Amen.

Here is a prayer that I composed for peace and harmony in the world. This prayer came to me one day when I was reflecting on what I could do to help bring peace and harmony into the world.

May the power, love and light of God be awakened
as peace, love and harmony in the minds and hearts
of all human beings, and particularly in those who in
the darkness of ignorance harbour harmful and negative
thoughts, words, and actions towards others.
May all human beings understand and value love,
kindness, compassion, forgiveness, and respect for
life. May all human beings cherish love over hatred,
and value non-violence, peace and harmony over
violence and disharmony.
Aum, Peace, Amen.

From the stillness of your meditation, visualise peace radiating out from you like ripples on a lake, in ever-expanding circles. Feel your peace is touching everything and everyone. Feel that you are expanding that feeling of peace farther and farther, beyond all limitations of your body and personality. See the whole planet with its blue aura floating in space, bathed in God's universal peace. See the Earth's surrounding aura filled with light, harmony, love, peace.

Then pray affirmatively: *"As I radiate God's peace, light, love and goodwill to others, I open the channel for God's love to flow through me."*

Visualise and feel that Cosmic Energy is surrounding and entering your body through the medulla oblongata (in the brain stem at the back of your head) and at your spiritual eye, flowing into your spine and down your arms into your hands. Then rapidly but gently rub your palms together until they feel warm and tingling with energy.

Raise your arms to the level of your head or above with your palms facing forward. Inhale deeply and then chant *Aum* as you exhale. You can chant *Aum* three times. Then say: *Aum Shanti, Peace, Amen* to end your prayer session. Take the divine qualities within you of *calmness*, *peace*, *love* and *joy* into your everyday life activities, and keep your awareness and connection to the Divine Presence. Realise that these divine qualities abide within your own being; they *are* you.

Effective Prayer by the universal law of attraction, we attract what we give attention, energy and focus to. For your prayers to be effective, turn your attention within to the calm, peaceful and still centre of your Being. Be present and aware in the stillness of your inner Self. By quietening your mind and being still, you can open yourself to experience the divine potential of energy and healing directly. God dwells within you as you. All things are in God as potentialities. There is a wellspring of creative and healing energy within us and the universe. By sharing in that creative process of the Divine, you can bring the unmanifest to manifestation. True prayer empowers us to know the Divine Presence as our changeless Source; it connects us to the Divine Presence.

Pray with clearly defined purpose. Keep in mind to allow situations to be resolved for the highest good of all. Give a prayer of appreciation or gratitude to confirm all of the blessings and positive things that are happening in your life right now.

When praying for other people or situations in the world – sending love, peace, healing, resolution, forgiveness – offer your prayers with positive words of truth with strong willpower and enthusiasm, knowing that energy follows thought. Avoid thinking or speaking about loss, lack, or limitation, as this will have a negative effect on your mind and prayer. Keep your thoughts, feelings, beliefs and attitudes in harmony with the Divine Mind. Have complete faith and confidence in the right and perfect outcome of your prayer.

Overcome the false sense of separation from God, by praying not to God but *in* God. Feel that you are immersed in the Divine Presence that is God, here and now, and allow that Light and Love to shine in and through you as you pray.

Understanding Your Mind

What Is the Mind?

The *Bhāgavad Gītā 7:4* confirms that the mind is of the subtle material nature. It is one of the eight primary elements (*ashta-prakritis*): earth, water, fire, air, ether, mind, intellect and ego. In the next verse of the *Bhāgavad Gītā 7:5*, it is stated that this material nature (mind, intellect, ego) is different from the highest nature of the Self.

> "The mind is not self-luminous because it is a
> perceptible object."
> Patañjali Yoga Sutra, 4:19.

The mind cannot explain itself, neither can it reveal the Self (pure Consciousness), because the Self transcends the mind and intellect. The Self is always the *witness* of the mind and senses, it is always the centre in all your activities, but as an instrument the mind can help to establish the Self by logic and reasoning. When the mind is purified, disciplined and stilled, then it becomes a useful instrument, but when in ignorance it falsely identifies with the body and senses it becomes a source of suffering and sorrow.

The great ancient sage, Patañjali who wrote the *Yoga Sūtras*, defined the mind as waves (*vṛttis*) on the ocean of Consciousness (*citta*), and that *Yoga* (union; unity; *samādhi* – total absorption) is the stilling of those waves (*yogaś citta vṛtti nirodhaḥ*). Yoga is the absolute stilling of the mind's activity, and to achieve Yoga is to abide in one's own true nature – the ever-present, Awareness-Consciousness (the changeless Self) – otherwise one identifies with the ego-self and experiences duality and separateness, and is limited by the ever-changing world through the incessant activity of the mind.

The mind is so fine and subtle that it cannot be distinguished from the Consciousness, the indwelling Self. It is transparent and reflects the Consciousness without distortion, and so it is difficult to distinguish mind from the Consciousness. In its true nature, this is what the mind really is – pure mind, filled with the luminous reflection of the pure Consciousness.

The body acts, the senses perceive, and the mind thinks and feels. The mind always functions in conjunction with the sense organs, without which neither forms nor thoughts can appear. Within all these activities, the changeless 'I'-principle (the centre of life) or Consciousness is found to be present, silently witnessing and knowing every one of them. *I am the witness or knower* of the body, the senses and the mind. Being separate from the body, senses and mind, *I am the witnessing Consciousness in all activities* (the ultimate *Knower* or *Perceiver*). Thought and feeling must have an object but Consciousness, the witnessing Self, has none, because the 'I'-principle is experience itself, and is beyond subject-object relationship. Consciousness is always your true centre, your *Being* in all activities; it is the *knowingness* that is never parted from you; it is the *Experiencer* who witnesses and knows the transient actions, perceptions, thoughts and feelings that flow in and out of the mind.

The Seat of the Mind

The mind is the seat of internal perception that has many different functions. The principle functions are cognition, volition, and emotion. The understanding, mind and intellect are all in the subtle body, they operate through corresponding centres in the physical brain. But the brain is *not* the mind, it is like a screen on which consciousness is reflected. The outer mind has its seat in the brain, through which it gains its experiences through the senses.

The inner subtle mind pervades throughout the body, but it has three main places in which it resides during the states of waking, deep sleep and dream. In the waking state, the mind resides at the eyebrow centre in the *ājñā chakra*. During deep sleep, the mind resides in a subtle state in the heart, *anāhata chakra*. In dream, it resides in the throat, *viśuddha chakra*. In dreamless sleep there are no thoughts; the distracting world of duality temporarily disappears. As soon as you awake from deep and dreamless sleep, you, the real Self continue to exist. You feel you existed even during deep sleep, because consciousness is continuous.

It is in the dreamless sleep state that we get a taste of the nature of absolute bliss. It is only the mind that creates differences, sorrow, duality and separateness.

The inner mind or feeling nature – your feelings, thoughts, sensations, memories and past impressions – is located in the heart (*hṛdaya*). It is this heart that makes you experience yourself as an individual with distinct characteristics and a personality.

Mind, Thoughts and Feelings

"The mind, coloured by countless latent tendencies,
comes to depend on things other than itself
owing to interactions with them."
Patanjali Yoga Sutra 4:24.

All objects, thoughts and feelings are known through the mind, but when these are absent, the mind cannot be said to exist. That which is existing beyond the mind is *Consciousness*, the changeless all-witnessing 'I'-principle.

Thoughts rise in Consciousness, exist in Consciousness and disappear in Consciousness, beyond the mind. When Consciousness is limited or objectified, then it is called thought. Just as waves are made of water, so thoughts are pure Consciousness.

Thoughts and feelings are like pictures projected on the background screen of the Self. To see the Self or Reality, the presence of thoughts and feelings must disappear, so that the mind is still.

We know that when the mind thinks, thoughts are constantly flowing in the mind. Whenever there are thoughts, the mind comes into existence, and when there are no thoughts, the mind ceases to exist. We also know that when our thoughts are calm, the mind is also calm. When the thoughts are restless, the mind is restless. In other words, the mind is coloured by the thoughts flowing through it.

This is like the relationship between water and a river. A pool of water is not a river, but when the water is flowing in a continuous stream, it becomes a river. Similarly, thought alone is not the mind. It is only when the thoughts are flowing that we can say that the mind exists. We can take this analogy further by saying that when the waters are flowing rapidly (as over rapids) the river is in a restless state. Similarly, as the thoughts become restless with desires, so the mind becomes restless. If the thoughts are negative, the mind becomes negative. Just as a cloth dipped in coloured dye takes on the colour in which it is dipped, so does the mind take on the qualities of the thoughts.

The Restless Mind

In the sixth chapter of the *Bhāgavad Gītā* (6:34), on the subject of meditation, Arjuna realises deep within himself that the mind cannot be stilled, and he says to Krishna, "The mind is restless, turbulent, strong and unyielding, I find it as difficult to control as the wind."

Krishna answers: *"O Mighty-armed Arjuna, without doubt, the mind is restless and difficult to control; but by practice (abhāsya) and by dispassion (vairāgya) it is restrained." (Bhāgavad Gītā 6:35).*

The mind's turbulence shows not only the speed in the flow of thoughts but also their restlessness and agitations. It is like a strong and powerful wind creating turbulence over the sea, causing uneven waves to rise and fall on the surface of the water.

When the mind is turbulent it is very difficult to calm, and when it becomes strongly attached to the objects of the senses or to a strong emotional feeling, or a negative thought, it is difficult to pull it or turn it away from its attachments. Also, if the mind has flown like the wind into a channel of its own choice, for the moment it is so unyielding that it is impossible to pull it back from its flight and persuade it to stay at the determined point of concentration.

In Chapter Three of the *Bhāgavad Gītā* (3.36), Arjuna asks this question: *"By what is one impelled, even against his will, to do wrong, constrained as it were by force?"*

We may also ask, what is it that makes the mind go astray? Why should it behave like this?

> *"By dwelling on the sense objects, a person develops an attachment to them. From attachment arises desire, and when desire is obstructed anger arises. From anger arises delusion. And from delusion comes forgetfulness of the Self, and from loss of memory comes the loss of the faculty of discrimination, resulting in annihilation of all right understanding."*
>
> *Bhāgavad Gīta (2:62–63)*

Krishna gives this answer: "*It is **desire**; it is **anger**, both of which are impelled by rajoguṇa* (quality of activity or passion). Desire and anger are related, because desire itself under certain circumstances, gains expression as anger. Desire is a constant agitation of the mind, expressing as an uncontrollable impatience to gain something or someone. When desire gets obstructed from attaining its desired object, frustration arises because the desire is unable to be fulfilled. Unsatisfied with the unfulfilled desire to obtain the object or person causes anger. When the powerful and violent force of anger arises, it gives us no time to discriminate, our memory wavers and we forget to discriminate wisely. This leads to the loss of reason and the forgetfulness of our true nature as the Self, resulting in a completely imbalanced mind.

Without pure reason one is unable to discriminate the truth from non-truth, the real from the unreal, the eternal from non-eternal.

Desire and Will

Desire and will are completely different from each other. Desire is a strong feeling of *wanting* or *longing* to have something or wishing for something to happen. Will is the power of *determination* without any motive whatsoever to enjoy anything. Mere wishing for the attainment of a desired thing will not be adequate; you will have to add to it a definite purpose. A wish or desire is only a small ripple in the mind-lake, whereas *will* is that power which puts into effect the desires. Will is volition – the power of choosing or determining.

When the Self determines the activity, uninfluenced by likes and dislikes towards surrounding objects, the *will* manifests. When likes and dislikes determine the activity and the person is pulled in various directions by them, unaware of the inner Reality – the Self – then *desire* manifests.

Desires can never be really fulfilled; they are only temporarily fulfilled. As soon as one desire has been temporarily satisfied, it is not long before the mind becomes restless again clamouring for satisfaction. It is a vicious cycle; restlessness creates desires, which creates further restlessness. These desires create deep active impressions (*saṁskāras*) in the subconscious mind. They are like seeds sown into the ground, and at the right time, they sprout and appear above the ground as a plant. These desire seed impressions or *saṁskāras* lie dormant deep in the mind; then, when the time or condition is right, they appear in the conscious mind as full-blown desires, creating a powerful urge within us to have them fulfilled and satisfied. If the desire is not satisfied then, one becomes frustrated and even angry.

> *"By dwelling on the sense objects, a person develops an attachment to them. From attachment arises desire, and when desire is obstructed anger arises. From anger arises delusion. And, from delusion comes forgetfulness of the Self, and from loss of memory comes the loss of the faculty of discrimination, resulting in annihilation of all right understanding."*
> *Bhāgavad Gītā 2:62–63*

Desire and anger are both impelled by *rajoguṇa* (quality of activity or passion). Desire and anger are related, because desire itself under certain circumstances gains expression as anger. Desire is a constant agitation of the mind, expressing as an uncontrollable impatience to gain something or someone. When desire gets obstructed from attaining its desired object, frustration arises because the desire is unable to be fulfilled. Unsatisfied with the unfulfilled desire to obtain the object or person causes anger.

When we are preoccupied only with seeking pleasure through sense-gratification, then there is a loss of will and desire to know the Truth, the reality of our true essential nature as the blissful, peaceful Self within us. The mind becomes dissipated and a slave to the senses. With such an unrestrained mind, there can be no inner peace, no true happiness and joy, and no spiritual fulfilment or success in concentration and meditation. It is only when your mind, senses, action and speech are disciplined, mastered and directed toward the spiritual goal that you can attain inner and outer freedom.

You, the spiritual Self, are an infinite *being* expressing as life through your material, physical mind, body and senses. All the negative and positive impulses that arise within you – desires, emotions and feelings – can be traced either to affirming your true nature or denial of it. All desires are our longing for the divine Self within, and until we look to the kingdom within, we will never find real happiness, for the external world is not the source of our spiritual fulfilment.

There is also a sense of wanting expansion of being to increase our joy, so what do we do? We add another body to us, we form a relationship, marry, and create a family, or we join a social network and gather lots of friends to us. The more we gain materially gives us a greater sense of expansion, but because it is all on the material level and concerned with the mind-body complex, it cannot be real and everlasting. For all that is born materially of this world is impermanent and will eventually leave us and pass away. Desire for attachment to what is impermanent causes pain and sorrow. Desires from which thoughts continuously flow into the mind disturb the reflection of the Truth in it.

As we continue through life with our preoccupation of gratifying our senses, seeking pleasure through our endless desires, and even seeking worldly knowledge, in trying to seek an everlasting happiness, some of us come to a point in our lives when we begin to think something is missing. Desires arise from our search from our own infinite Divinity, our true eternal nature, the God-Self within. Outwardly, in the world we are all seeking Truth of our spiritual nature, we became convinced that the fundamental reality is material, so we erroneously started to realise this infinite Being through matter, and therefore it became distorted.

Latent Impression (*saṁskāra*)

Every experience or past thoughts, feelings, perceptions and actions forms an imprint in the mind, and influences your subsequent activities. Your *desires* leave an impression deep within the mind, and they sprout, creating an impulse within you to repeat the same experience of which they were impressions. In Sanskrit and Yoga terminology, these impressions are called *saṁskāra*. The *saṁskāra* identified as thoughts, desires, and tendencies in the mind which lead to action and reaction can be compared to a garden in which seeds have been planted. Without the right soil and weather conditions, the seeds remain dormant. Similarly, *saṁskāra* also remain dormant if they are not connected with the mind, senses and objects. As soon as a dormant seed becomes activated by the warmth of the soil and is watered by the rain, it begins to grow. Similarly, *saṁskāra* wait for an opportunity to manifest: a recollection of pleasure, a memory of a sensation from something that gave us momentary satisfaction can occupy and churn the mind. This is the latent or dormant *karmic* impression, a *saṁskāra*, that like a seed, has been watered, has been activated, and has pushed its way up into our awareness from deep within our subconscious mind. The mind becomes restless with this *saṁskāric* thought, creating desire and attachment and forming a habit by the impulse within it to repeat the same pleasurable experience. The greater the attachment the stronger the *saṁskāra* it creates.

The more powerful and deeply embedded *saṁskāras* are known as *vāsanās*, which means 'colouring'. *Vāsanās* are your unmanifested tendencies that colour the mind affecting your desires, feelings, thoughts and intentions; they shape your mind and colour it, and dominate it, and create your character and life. When this happens your thoughts, speech and actions become conditioned by your *vāsanās*. Their roots are so deeply embedded in the soil of the mind that they dictate how and what you think, without you even being aware of it. A vicious cycle is set up in which thoughts to subtle karmic impressions and from subtle karmic impressions to thoughts continuously revolve.

It is only when these *vāsanās* are exhausted, that the mind automatically becomes quiet. It is only in a quiet mind that peace and happiness is experienced. *Vāsanās* control your thoughts, which in turn creates your actions. By changing your thoughts, you can change your life. When a negative thought enters your mind, immediately and totally reject it, and substitute an opposite positive thought. Never leave your mind idle, weak or vacant. To prevent negative and useless thoughts from invading your mind, fill your mind with positive and optimistic thoughts, and creative ideas, that will create good habits to purify and transform your mind both mentally and spiritually, bringing you inner and outer fulfilment and true happiness. When the *saṁskāras* of your real nature become strong enough to subdue the old ones by their very presence, desires will no longer tempt you away from the Truth.

Habits

"Change the trend of your thoughts – cast out all negative mental habits. Replace them with wholesome, courageous thought habits, and apply them in daily life with unshakable confidence."

Paramhansa Yogananda ('How to Be a Success', *The Wisdom of Yogananda*, Volume 4, 2008. Crystal Clarity Publishers, Nevada City, CA 95959).

The lives of most persons are not governed by weak resolutions, but by *habits*. These lifetime habits are ingrained in us; they create imbalance and disharmony within us. Habits also create addictions, that temporarily give us a sense of comfort, but ultimately, they disempower us; we lose our wise discrimination and will power. Addiction is a symptom of a much deeper problem that a person struggles to deal with and suffers from. An addictive pattern can be a long and difficult process to get out of. Those who fall under the power of addictive habits become enslaved by them – drugs, alcohol, smoking and sex can enslave the will to the body. The will power becomes weak. Drugs and alcohol paralyse the will. Without the power of the will, Self-realisation is not possible. It is the *will power* and enthusiastic *energy* that keeps us moving forward to achieve our worthy goals and to accomplish them successfully. When there is a lack of enthusiasm, there is no will. Remember, *energy* and *will* go together. To develop your will, you have to discipline your mind and eradicate reluctance to give up bad habits – moods, anger, wrong attitudes, likes and dislikes – that are controlling you and holding you back in your lower nature. Renounce the undesirable tendencies of the mind, and hold to those great virtues – courage, determination, perseverance, patience and concentration – that strengthen your mind and uplift your spirit go give you unshakable balance through all the challenges of daily life. To strengthen your will, perform all your actions with discipline and renounce the illusions of the world.

A habit is an acquired habitual behaviour, thought pattern, or old belief that one repeats so many times that it becomes almost unconscious. The behaviour is so ingrained in us that we act without thinking about what we are saying or doing. Most of the time we engage in habits without thinking, which can either be helpful or harmful. In a positive and beneficial sense, the formation of a good habit enables you to act automatically on 'auto-pilot', freeing up time and energy for you to focus on other things that need your special attention. In a negative sense, bad habits can cause problems in your personal life and affect others. They can cause mental and physical ill health, they waste time and energy and they prevent you from accomplishing your worthy goals in life.

These bad habits are not only the obvious habits, such as habitually biting your nails, eating the wrong foods or overeating, or smoking, but include psychological or mental bad habits such as procrastination, gossiping, thinking negatively, resisting change, negatively criticising and being judgemental towards others.

Changing Negative Habits

*"Powerful bad habits can be displaced by opposite good
habits if the latter are patiently cultured. First crowd
out all bad habits by good habits in everything, then
cultivate the consciousness of being free from all habits."*
Paramhansa Yogananda ('How to Awaken Your True Potential', *The Wisdom
of Yogananda*, Volume 7, 2015. Crystal Clarity Publishers, Nevada City, CA
95959).

To overcome a bad habit, the first thing you need to do is ask yourself: What is
missing from life? What gap in my life am I trying to fill by doing this habit? Is
boredom, loneliness, or stress a factor involved? Or is there something deeper
that is causing you to hold on to something that is bad for you? Perhaps a fear,
an event, or a limiting belief?

Some deeply rooted habits or beliefs may take longer to eliminate from
your consciousness. This habitual energy that has lingered from the past can
resurface and throw you off balance, distracting and stressing you. Remember
that you have come to your present condition through errors and mistakes
lasting lifetimes, so do not expect in one day, or one week, or even one month
to root out old beliefs and old and tenacious bad habits, and break free from the
cyclic force of habitual activity. It can take time to destroy old habits and
replace them with new fresh ideas, creating good habits. If you are to conquer
the foe of bad habits that drive you to act in ways to maintain suffering, then
you must banish them completely from the kingdom of your mind, and
establish the rightful ruler, the indwelling divine Self, on the throne to guide
you with wisdom and understanding. This is where you will need self-
discipline, commitment to practice (*abhyāsa*), non-attachment, dispassion
(*Vairāgya*), patience, *will power* and a strong persistent perseverance,
willingness and resolve to succeed. Then gradually you will find that the
positive and good habits will begin to influence your life in a beneficial way,
and on all levels – physical, mental and spiritual.

Methods of Overcoming Bad Habits

*"When the habit of delusion precedes the habit of wisdom
and settles in the soul, the only way out is to use will power
to meditate deeply and daily until the all-alluring, bliss-
contact of God is definitely achieved and can be reproduced
in the consciousness at will."*
Paramhansa Yogananda ('How to Awaken Your True Potential', *The Wisdom
of Yogananda*, Volume 7, 2015. Crystal Clarity Publishers, Nevada City, CA
95959).

To weaken an old or bad habit, avoid everything that arouses and stimulates it. Divert the attention of your mind towards a good positive habit and cultivate it by the strength of your *willpower* and the power of deep concentration. In other words, neutralise bad habits by creating good habits. Meditate daily more deeply to erase the pattern of bad habits and tendencies. Strive always with your greatest *effort* to resist and overcome any bad habits or tendencies to wrong thoughts and actions, but be *patient,* as it may take time. As you meditate longer and more deeply, develop your powers of discrimination, and make an effort to overcome your bad habits; you may find when you least expect it, a great burden has been lifted from your consciousness freeing you from the tenacious grip of a bad habit or tendency. Imagine the joy and lightness of being that brings – to be free of a negative habit.

Sit quietly and peacefully in a seated meditation posture that is comfortable for you, with your head, neck and spine aligned upright. Then, centring yourself within, relax and free your mind from all worries and restlessness. Then pray earnestly and with devotion:

'Heavenly Father grant me the wisdom to discriminate wisely. Strengthen my will power to conquer and defeat all wrong tendencies and bad habits in me. May Your Divine Light reveal the errors in my consciousness and dissolve them completely. Lead me from the darkness of ignorance to the Light of Your Supreme Consciousness in Truth and eternal Joy.'

Now concentrating deeply at the command centre (*Ājñā Chakra* – midpoint between the eyes on the forehead), the spiritual eye, the centre of *will power*, meditate for a few minutes. Then using any of the affirmations below, with firm intention, sincerity and deep *attention*, say it first aloud, then softly, then fading into a whisper and finally affirm mentally with faith and conviction, so that the affirmation carries its meaning deep down into the subconscious:

As I follow my true inner wisdom and guidance, I identify false, harmful, and destructive habits, and drive them out of my mind, and change what needs to be changed. I now release old patterns, habits, and beliefs and replace them with fresh new positive thoughts. I am strong, confident and courageous to overcome all useless thoughts and habits. I let go and release from my consciousness all that is not needed. As I let go of old binding habits, I make space in my consciousness to fill it with positive, wise, and divine thoughts and ideas that help me to grow in understanding, love, wisdom and truth. I experience true freedom as I awaken to my spiritual nature. I hold this truth in my mind.

My mind is like a garden; I uproot the weeds of bad thoughts and bad habits and eliminate them. Creating space in my mind-garden, I plant and cultivate beautiful fresh and new positive thoughts and good habits. I nourish my beautiful garden of consciousness by connecting in deep meditation with the Divine Consciousness. So that blooms of love unfold their beauty and life in me.

I relax and cast aside all old patterns, habits and beliefs, allowing new positive and divine thoughts to take their place.

The best time to repeat affirmations with deep concentration is when you awake first thing in the morning when you are feeling fresh and alert from a good night's sleep, and last thing at night just before falling asleep. At these times, the subconscious mind is more receptive to receiving such positive affirmations.

Six Important Powers of the Mind

The six important powers of the mind are:

1. **The power of cognition.** The power of perception, knowing and understanding through thought, experience and the senses.

2. **The power of memory.** To remember, recollect and recognise. This power grasps and takes possession of perceptions and judgements; it holds and brings to memory whenever a fact is needed. Memories are the reactivation of the imprints (*saṁskāra*) of sense objects that one has experienced and recognised in the past.

3. **The power of imagination.** The action of forming new ideas, or images or concepts of external objects not present to the senses. Everything imagined or dreamed is imprinted on the subconscious mind and leaves a lasting impression (*saṁskāra*).

4. **The power of judgement.** Comparing, contrasting, drawing inferences on the basis of evidence and reasoning, discussing and concluding. Ascertainment and logical reasoning are its subdivisions.

5. **Willpower.** Control deliberately exerted to do something or to restrain one's own impulses. The faculty by which a person decides on and

initiates action. By converting your thoughts into *will power* and will into action, you can achieve your goals. *Will power* is greater than imagination because what would imagination do without the impelling power of the will to execute with its dynamic power, desires, wishes and ideals?

6. **The power to hold steady.** The power to hold steady is really a part of memory. When you have the power to hold it means you have fixed and steady ideas that cannot be changed by anyone; an unwavering mind. Holding a thought with determined *will power* means holding to it until that thought pattern develops dynamic force. When you have unwavering one-pointed attention, stillness is reached.

Will Power

"The supreme will power belongs to consciousness,
Not to the ego or personal self. That supreme
Will power arises through aligning ourselves
With the Divine will and inherent power
of existence."
David Frawley.
('The Art and Science of Vedic Counselling'
   –David Frawley and Suhas Kshirsagar)

Will power is one of the six important powers of the mind. Paramhansa Yogananda gave this definition of will power: *"Will power is that which changes thought into energy."* In other words, this means convert your thoughts into *will power* and your will into action. *Will* is the dynamo of existence; without it, evolution is impossible. By using your power of will, you can apply it to a thought giving it tremendous energy to transform something, so that it takes place. With *will power* and *self-discipline,* you can accomplish great things; these are two powerful keys to success in life that move and make things happen and creates things that are worthwhile. There is nothing impossible of achievement for a person of strong will with self-discipline. Successful individuals who accomplish things in life are those who are self-disciplined and have developed their will, discrimination and understanding. They set the right intention and goal to achieve something, and once that is set, no amount of obstacles can stop them from achieving their goal. No matter how many times they fall, they never give up, they always rise to try again and with an indomitable will power succeed.

Yet for many of us even the smallest task, challenge, petty desires or temptation can defeat our power of will.

What Is Will?

Will implies self-determination. There cannot be self-determination without self-awareness. In the states of dream, drowsiness and being intoxicated, the will does not function because of the vagueness of self-awareness. In those states in which one has no self-control only unrestrained emotion and imagination prevail.

What Is Will Power?

"Desires, plus energy, produce will power.
The will directs the energy to flow either
Upward or downward depending on
whether the desire directing it is
positive or negative. The energy-flow
facilitates, without defining, the
direction of consciousness. Even so, an
upward flow of energy increases the
feeling of happiness."
Swami Kriyananda ('God is For Everyone')

Will power is the inner strength that boosts your self-confidence, enabling you to overcome obstacles, difficulties and challenges in life, and to overcome harmful habits. Will power gives you the ability to delay gratification and resist short-term temptations in order to meet long-term goals. You cannot think without *willing* to think and you cannot act without *willing* to act. Will power pushes you towards goals, success and achievement. It gives you the inner power and *energy* to take action and to perform any task or plan. With *will power,* you have the *energy* to lift yourself out of laziness and procrastination, for when there is will power, there is also a focused determination, perseverance, and resolution to succeed, regardless of inner resistance, difficulties or discomfort. A person with strong will power has the capacity to override unwanted thoughts, feelings or impulses and is able to assert decisions even in the face of strong opposition, whereas a person with weak energy and little will power gives in easily. Those who do not exercise their will power are easily influenced and controlled by their environment. Paramhansa Yogananda said, *"Environment is stronger than will power."* Unless your wisdom-guided will power is stronger, your environment can tempt and seduce you, forming bad habits in you.

Obstacles to Will Power

Procrastination

Procrastination is to postpone, defer ('put to one side') or avoid something that must or needs to be done, often because it seems boring or unpleasant. When we procrastinate, we avoid doing a task or something that needs to be accomplished, whether it be an appointment to see the dentist or doctor, to face up and deal with a problem or difficult situation, or to sit for meditation. If procrastination is not overcome, it can lead to stress, and feelings of inadequacy, self-doubt, guilt and low self-esteem.

Laziness and unwillingness are connected with procrastination.

How to Overcome Procrastination:
- Be aware of your thoughts and habits that lead to procrastination.
- Discipline yourself to the priorities you set.
- Set realistic goals.
- Keep yourself motivated.
- Be positive, energetic and enthusiastic.
- Practice Yogananda's *Energisation Exercises*
- Practice Swami Kriyananda's *Superconscious Living Exercises*
- Tackle one problem at a time and enjoy the small successes of achievement.

Affirmation: *I possess the wisdom, will power, motivation, inspiration and the energy to accomplish anything and everything. I can do whatever I set my mind to, no matter how difficult or challenging the task is. I am willing to tackle difficult challenges. I value integrity and get done what I have promised myself to do. I keep my goal constantly present in my mind and overcome any resistance to it. I act now.*

Laziness

*"Idleness is extremely detrimental to spiritual
realisation. Laziness in body or mind must
be driven away before you can emerge
to the kingdom of God."*

Paramhansa Yogananda.

'How to Awaken Your True Potential', *The Wisdom of Yogananda*, Volume 7,
Paramhansa Yogananda, Crystal Clarity Publishers, Nevada City, California.
(2010)

Laziness is a habit that may reflect a decreased level of motivation, boredom and a lack interest in an activity. There is also a lack of enthusiasm, effort and energy in laziness, as well as unwillingness.

A lazy person may have a reluctance to work or make an effort to meditate. A person could also have a complacency – a feeling of smug or uncritical satisfaction with oneself or one's achievements – and feel that they do not need to work or meditate.

Another word for laziness is 'sloth' (a slow-moving tropical American mammal that hangs upside down from the branches of a tree). A lazy sloth-like person clings to inactivity, procrastination, with no effort or enthusiasm to do anything.

A lack of motivation and not knowing what to do with your life can also be factors in laziness and lethargy. Being lethargic or unproductive is ultimately just a habit, so by breaking out of your old habit patterns and creating new ones, you will be more motivated to find something more fulfilling. You could start by making a checklist of the desires, goals and motivations you want to move towards, this will help you to stay focused and motivated. Keep your sights focused on the goals you have set yourself and be solution orientated. Regularly assess both the importance and value of the problem or goal so that you keep focused. Remember, you are always in a position to choose and reinvent yourself and make change happen.

Those people who appear lazy often repeat the same negative statements, 'I don't want to', 'I can't', 'I'm not interested', or other self-limiting beliefs. Each time a limiting belief is repeated, it reinforces the limitation. To counteract these limiting beliefs, use positive affirmations and positive statements. Change the 'I can't' to 'I can'.

Strengthen your motivation through positive affirmations, visualisation and thinking about the importance of your goals.

Develop your will power, be disciplined and don't give up, make a greater effort day by day to overcome your difficulties. Yogananda said, "Each day, strive to accomplish something that you have always thought you could not accomplish."

Affirmation: *I am fully energised and motivated to take action and do anything that I have or want to do. With will and energy, I am free from laziness, and I am open to limitless possibilities.*

Restlessness

*"Never let your mind be seduced by restlessness,
through joking too much, too many distractions
and so on. Be deep. As soon as you succumb to
restlessness, all the old troubles will begin to
exert their pull on the mind once again:
sex, wine and money."*
Paramhansa Yogananda.
The Wisdom of Yogananda, Volume 5, Paramhansa
Yogananda, Crystal Clarity Publishers, Nevada City, California. (2010)

Mental restlessness is caused by strong desires, likes or dislikes, negative thoughts and ambition. Restlessness is also a common symptom of anxiety. It is the feeling of discontentment, being unable to sit still, your attention is distracted by all kinds of thoughts; you are unable to focus or concentrate. Or it can be the feeling as though you are on edge and something is about to or needs to happen. When we have constant thoughts of discontent, worry, fear, melancholy, anger hatred and resentment, a lack of purpose in life, the mind becomes restless.

Over-excitement can also cause restlessness by upsetting the balance of the nervous system.

How to Overcome Restlessness

First, ask yourself what's going on in your life that could be causing the restless feelings. Why am I feeling this way? It may be a signal that something wrong is going on. Try to understand why you are feeling restless. Put your thoughts or worries to paper – write them down, so you can get them out of your head and see them objectively and more clearly. By first acknowledging your own mental chatter, you can move away from it.

Practice the following practices to relax and calm your body–breath–mind;

Practice Yogananda's *'Tense with will, relax and feel'* exercise;

Breathe in with a double breath through your nose, and while holding the breath in, tense all the muscles in your body, and feel the energy vibrating in all the body parts, energising and revitalising.

Then exhale the breath, *relax* the tension, and *feel* the energy and vitality in the recharged muscles. In *feeling* the energy, feel that you are not the physical body but that you are the life which sustains the body. Mental peace is attained when the body is relaxed and calm.

Restless feelings can be calmed by conscious breathing. Here is a simple breathing exercise to the ratio of 6:6:6;

Inhale through the nostrils to a slow count of **six**;

Hold the breath in for count of **six**;

Exhale slowly to the count of **six**.

Practice nine rounds of the 6:6:6 breathing, then sit quiet and still, and with your eyes closed with your attention at the point between the eyebrows on the forehead, practice the *Hong-Sau Technique* (see page 111), which calms the mind and deepens concentration.

In that inner calmness, you will find peace and happiness within yourself.

Affirmation: *I relax and let go of all restless thoughts and feelings. I replace restlessness with calm confidence and steady courage. I am peaceful and calm; my thoughts and feelings are in harmony.*

Unwillingness

When a person is unwilling or reluctant to say, give or do something, there is a 'holding back' or a resistance, a reluctance with a lack of enthusiasm. One is not fully committed to act.

The source of unwillingness is the mind, and unwillingness is one of the main obstacles to strong will power. Unwillingness develops very slowly inside us, and it can be very destructive. You will never be successful if you are unwilling for to be successful in life you need to have the *will* and *energy*, interest and enthusiasm, courage and determination to become the person you envision yourself to be. You need willingness to create the life you want.

Unwillingness can apply to different situations such as: unwilling to forgive, unwilling to work, unwilling to meditate, unwilling to make an effort and so on.

Willingness requires effort, energy and enthusiasm. For example, waking up on a cold dark winter morning, you may not feel the enthusiasm and willingness to sit for meditation. Perhaps, you would rather spend that extra hour in bed. In comparison, a person with willingness, enthusiasm, will power and energy will feel eager to meditate no matter what conditions arise. He or she will have an inner strength that overcomes all difficulties.

How to Overcome Unwillingness

Be *motivated* and take *interest* in everything you do. Motivation is essential to creativity, productivity and happiness. Motivation is what causes us to act, and when we act, we create movement, growth and change. Motivation can make us feel involved and significant; it can help us to create more of what we want in our lives. This gives us meaning and purpose in our lives, which leads to happiness.

Paramhansa Yogananda said, "*The greater the will, the greater the flow of energy.*" This means that when you truly have the willingness (with a strong feeling) to do something, perform an action, or get something done, there is no thought of *I can't* or *I won't*, there is no resistance to obstruct the flow of energy. The will becomes strong and focused and attracts the support of energy to magnetise you and strengthen your efforts. It is the *will* power that directs the energy. So, it is important to develop your willingness by not giving in to defeat when challenges and difficulties arise, but to remain calm with your full attention focused on your goal, to be determined to succeed and to persevere with a positive attitude. As Yogananda said, *"A strong will, by its dynamic force, creates a way for its fulfilment."*

Each time you are faced with a difficult situation or challenge, instead of seeing it as an insurmountable obstacle and creating a resistance to it, welcome it as an opportunity to use your courage and will power to summon up the energy to overcome it.

Doubt and failure should not enter your mind; once your will is strong, and you are focused and determined to succeed, there should be no turning back. Never give up; persevere until you succeed.

To increase your energy flow practise Swami Kriyananda's *Superconscious Living Exercises* (see page 104) and Paramhansa Yogananda's *Energisation Exercises* (see page 082).

Affirmation: *I have the motivation, enthusiasm, will and energy to do anything that I need to do. Each time, I am faced with a difficult challenge, I welcome it as an opportunity to use my willingness, courage and will power to overcome it.*

Fear

"Fear is destructive to mental initiative, courage, judgement, common sense and will power. Fear shrouds the soul's all-conquering confidence and power."
Paramhansa Yogananda.
The Wisdom of Yogananda, Volume 5, Paramhansa

Yogananda, Crystal Clarity Publishers, Nevada City, California. (2010)

The greatest of all fears that everyone can experience at some time in their life is the fear of death. Fear of death can relate to one's own death, the death of others (friends, relatives, loved ones and others in general), of the dying process (fear of a slow or painful death) and fear of the unknown after death. Fear of old age, growing old is also related because death of the body is certain for everybody.

Fear and anxiety thrive when we imagine the worst. Fear of the 'unknown', or irrational fear, which is always projected into the future, can cause anxiety. From the point of view of irrational fear, it can slow you down, and make you hesitant and careful, cause you to lose motivation and prevent you from going forward.

The more common fears are when you become anxious and fear upcoming events such as an interview, having to give a speech, going to the dentist, or when you have to face up to or deal with a difficult person, problem or situation. There is also fear of responsibility, failure and illness, which is created by constantly thinking and worrying about dire consequences. And there is the fear of being different and being separated from friends and family. The stronger the fear becomes, the more likely that it will draw to you the very things you most fear.

How to Overcome Fear

To deal with fear, start by naming your fears; bring them out into the open. Question your fears by writing them down on paper: "Why am I afraid of that happening? What are the chances that would really happen?"

Banish fear from your mind by refusing to be afraid; do not allow it to become a subconscious habit that asserts itself and disempowers you. Affirm aloud, softly and then mentally: "God is my Source, my strength, my courage and my power. Divine light shines through every problem and circumstance, dissolving any obstacles and comforting my heart. I am always safe and secure with and in God."

As an eternal spiritual being, know that death has no more reality for you than it had for the great spiritual Masters: Jesus Christ, Mahavatar Babaji, Lahiri Mahasaya, Swami Sri Yukteswar and Paramhansa Yogananda. Death is merely a doorway through which we pass to continue our spiritual journey elsewhere in the Oneness that is God.

Through daily meditation, prayer and affirmations, keep your attention on the Divine presence within you for when your attention and awareness are wholly on the Divine presence within, there is no room for fearful thoughts. Maintaining your spiritual practices of meditation and prayer keeps you open to the flow of divine ideas, wisdom and guidance. It gives you the inner strength, will power and courage to overcome fear and other obstacles in your life. It gives you inner peace and contentment, and a sense of purpose to direct you in life.

Affirmation: *I let go of any sense of fear that may have limited my journey forward or caused procrastination. I remind myself that I am not alone. God and I are one.*

Paramhansa Yogananda said that fear comes from the heart and that if ever you feel overcome by fear, you should breathe deeply and rhythmically several times, relaxing with each exhalation.

When fear and anxiety take a hold of you, it is impossible to think clearly, so the first the first thing to do is distract your mind from worrying by physically calming down. Stop, and focus on your breath. Place the palm on your abdomen and breathe slowly and deeply concentrating on each breath. Breathe in steadily through your nose for a count of five and out through your mouth for a count of ten, feeling that you are breathing out the fear and relaxing with each exhalation. Keep doing this for three to five minutes. Fear and anxiety cause the breath to become rapid and shallow; so, by consciously controlling your breathing, you control the anxiety symptoms.

After breathing deeply and rhythmically, use your will power to divert the mind from all thoughts of fear by turning your attention away from worrying thoughts to the inner calmness and peace of the true divine Self within you. Sit quietly, calm your senses and thoughts, concentrate at the spiritual eye (point in the forehead between the eyebrows) and meditate deeply.

Affirmation: *I know that fear is an illusion and I will not let it paralyse me. I have nothing to fear, the guiding Light of God is within me and around me.*

Indecisiveness

Indecisiveness is not having or showing the ability to make decisions quickly and effectively. Indecisiveness results from a failure to make a choice between alternatives.

Hesitation can be either due to fear (not *being* prepared or capable) or anxiety (not *feeling* prepared or capable). You may be afraid to make a mistake, afraid to be wrong, or afraid to make a decision and act on it. It is one thing to be cautious, but to fear can have a paralysing effect that leads to a no-action decision.

Being decisive is about making choices, measuring feedback and acting on it. When making a decision, you have to be very clear on what you are trying to achieve, why you are trying to achieve it and how you plan on achieving it. When you know your purpose in life and have a clear vision of your long-term vision, all the smaller, day-to-day decisions will become much easier. You will be guided intuitively in the right direction. When it comes to making difficult choices, one of the most valuable resources lies within you. Your *intuition*, which is a powerful indicator of the right choice. Intuition is developed through deep meditation in which the mind becomes clear and calm.

An indecisive person's mind is usually restless, so to make clear and right decisions one needs to have a calm mind. Making the right choices is a natural expression of wisdom that is dependent on harmony within, reflected in calmness of the mind.

How to Overcome Indecision

If it is fear that is stopping you from making a decision, then ask yourself, "What is the worst scenario or outcome that could happen from making this decision?" The scenario or outcome is possible but is not assured. Remember, no matter what your challenges are; you are not too weak to overcome them. So make a decision! Do not let fear paralyse you into a no-action decision.

Yogananda's guru, Swami Sri Yukteswar said, "*Look fear in the face and it will cease to trouble you*".

If you need more time to make an important decision, meditate deeply until your mind is calm and clear and then pray for the right outcome. Be intuitively guided to make the right decision from the insights you have gained in meditation and prayer.

Affirmation: *I take charge of my life and with confidence and trust, and guided by my intuition, I always choose in making the wise and right decisions.*

Lack of Concentration

Without concentration, the energy of the mind becomes scattered, diffused and unfocused. This causes the mind to be inattentive, distracted and disturbed, resulting in the mind being unable to fulfil its true potential.

Concentration is the ability to withdraw the mind from objects of distraction and hold or fix its attention on one object, or one thing, or one idea at a time.

Attention and concentration are necessary in all actions if we are to achieve anything successfully and safely. The more you can apply your attention and concentration in everyday life, the greater will be your success in meditation.

Meditation begins with concentration, for to enter the state of superconscious meditation the mind must become calm, steady and one-pointed. Concentration is the key that opens the door to meditation.

There can be no concentration without *interest* and *attention*; they are interdependent. Interest develops attention, and attention is needed for concentration.

Attention is of two kinds, voluntary and involuntary. When we direct our attention towards an object by determined effort of the will, it is called voluntary attention. Involuntary attention is when there is no effort of the will – we see a beautiful sunset or a beautiful object and our attention is naturally and spontaneously drawn to it.

The difficulty in understanding the term 'concentration' in the yogic sense is that, commonly, concentration is associated with mental effort and tenseness. One concentrates in order to defend, possess or achieve something. In this sense, concentration is ego-motivated; it is an outward effort of the will, charged with the energy of the feelings, instead of a *steady effortless flow of will power*.

How to Develop Concentration

• Eliminate distractions

Concentrate on one thing at a time. Stop multitasking; it interferes with the ability to learn and, especially, to remember. If you do two or more things at the same time, you are dividing your attention and not giving it one hundred percent of your focus to the task. Do not be side-tracked by interruptions or mind wandering.

Even when you are practising Yogananda's *Energisation Exercises*, they should be practised one-pointedly with no distracting thoughts. Your mind should be calmly focused with concentration on the exercises.

• Cultivate attentiveness

Attentiveness is cultivated from the more you notice. It is developing an eye for detail, noticing the little things and the unnoticed things that other people do not notice. By being attentive and noticing details, you will also develop your memory.

As a tourist, you may be walking in a foreign city that you are not familiar with and you may get lost. If you were walking from your hotel to a tourist attraction in the city, that may be quite straightforward, but if you were to walk back to your hotel it may not be so easy to find, especially if you had not paid any attention to visual details – landmarks, street names, buildings, shops, etc. – that create a memory-map in your mind.

Remember, *attention* and *memory* are two important mental skills and are directly related. In fact, many memory complaints have nothing to do with the actual ability to remember things. They come from a failure to focus properly on the task at hand. Many of our actions are performed automatically, this is why we need to cultivate focused attention and ignore distraction.

• Set aside time to deal with worries

There are many people who have trouble in concentrating during the day because they are constantly worrying about other things, causing the attention to become distracted and divided. So if you find yourself distracted by worries, download the worries from your mind by noting them down on paper. In this way, you will not retain them in your mind. Then schedule time to deal with the worrying issues.

• Remain present in the now moment

The more you are centred in your calm inner Self and present in each *now* moment the more you are able to focus your attention and concentrate. We exist in the present, but when we think, we either think of the past or the future, for there is no thought in the present. Even the thought about the future is based on the experiences of the past and therefore it is modified past. Thought is moving from the past to the present and from the present to the future, without even resting for a moment in the present, like the movement of a pendulum to and fro. We may live 100 years, but actual life, the actual existence of which we become aware of at any given moment is the new, the present. We may think of tomorrow, but when tomorrow arrives we become aware of it only as today not as tomorrow. Life is *now*, yesterday and tomorrow are thoughts and imagination. Therefore, to understand life, observe it and enjoy it, we have to give our whole attention to it today, now at the present moment.

• Prioritise

When you have too many tasks to complete, it can be distracting and overwhelming, you lose your attention and concentration, and this sometimes can also cause procrastination. When you are not sure which tasks to start or which are most important, take ten or fifteen minutes to make a priority list.

To maximise your concentration, do your hardest task when you are most alert.

• Take short breaks

You may find it a struggle to focus and concentrate on tasks for hours at a time, so divide your time into smaller segments, by inserting a five to 15-minute break between tasks, to give your mind a rest. You can do this by taking a brisk walk in the fresh air whilst breathing deeply; then you can return to your task recharged with energy feeling more alert to focus with your attention.

• Stay calm

When your energy is scattered it also restless. A scattered and restless energy is unable to focus; there is no attention or concentration. For deep concentration, the mind needs to be calm. When the mind is calm and focused in concentration the will can more easily direct its energy into *will power*.

• Increase and control your energy

Practise Yogananda's *Energisation Exercises*. When these exercises are practised with calm focus, they will help you to cultivate concentration that will increase your energy and control any scattering or restlessness of the mind.

• Meditate

Practise the *Hong-Sau Technique* (see page 127). This technique is one of the best meditation techniques for calming the mind and for deepening the concentration.

Affirmation: *Total concentration is mine. I have the power to focus my concentration at will. I remain alert and focused. My focus is clear, my attention flows to one thing at a time.*

Low self-esteem – feelings of inadequacy

Low self-esteem is having a lack of self-confidence in one's own worth or abilities, it is seeing oneself as inadequate, unworthy, unacceptable, incompetent, and unlovable. If you believe in such negative self-critical beliefs, it can affect your behaviour and your life decisions and choices, leaving you feeling unaccepted and unfulfilled.

The delusion of thinking you cannot change at will, seeing yourself as being weak or a failure, and hopelessly remaining a victim of circumstances of the past, weakens your will power. You lose heart and become discouraged, and you lose confidence and enthusiasm.

Self-esteem is interchangeable with confidence, self-worth, self-belief, and self-love. Self-esteem means believing in yourself, knowing that you are doing the best you know how. It means living by your beliefs and values no matter what others say and do.

How to Overcome Low Self-Esteem

• Be present in the moment

When you are living from your true divine nature that is eternally present, you are at peace, relaxed, content, and absorbed, with no ego-thoughts about *me* or *my story*. By living focused on the moment, you can choose your actions consciously and wisely, unaffected by worries of lack, and inability to deal with situations or with life.

• Cultivate awareness

It is through being consciously aware, that you can recognise how you are responding and reacting to your self-limiting fears. The more you notice the effect that paying attention to your thoughts has on you – stress, fear, tension, negative thoughts and feelings – the more you will be able to turn your attention away and remain calmly present in the moment.

By creating a relaxed moment of mental quiet in which you are in *awareness* you are then able to choose to respond from your true Self rather than the ego.

• Be non-judgemental

When you stop judging and criticising yourself (and others) and simply accept yourself, including your experiences, failures and successes, you will live more consciously in your true nature, which has the essential characteristics of freedom, happiness, peace, acceptance, contentment and joy.

Let go of fear

'Do not be afraid; do not be discouraged, for the
Lord your God is with you wherever you go.'
The Bible, Joshua 1:9

A life mainly guided by fear has a contracting effect on us. Fear is aroused to warn you of imminent danger so that you may defend and protect yourself from that danger. It can be a stimulus to right action, with awareness and focus, or it may cause you to react in paralysis – you may not act at all.

It is only by feeling fear totally and understanding its source can you learn the purpose of that particular fear you are experiencing and gain an understanding of how it is not a part of your true essential nature. Learning to become mindful of your thoughts in the present moment is a positive step toward letting go of fearful thoughts. When you are worrying, it is either about the past or about the future, you cannot worry in the present.

Whenever fearful thoughts enter your mind, notice that they are thoughts created by your mind and not necessarily facts that are true. Allow yourself to have such thoughts without reacting on them (your reaction to your thoughts starts repetitiveness and obsessing), accept those thoughts in the moment, and let them go.

Your thoughts do not define who you are because they are just thoughts. It is through identifying yourself with the ego mind that you believe in the self-created image and labels of yourself. Observe your thoughts for what they are: just thoughts, they come, and they go, like moving clouds in the sky. Your true essential nature like the clear sky is unaffected by thoughts.

Affirmation: *I love, honour and respect myself unconditionally at all times. I radiate love and respect and in return, I receive love and respect. I believe in myself. My feelings of self-worth fill me with enthusiasm. I am inspired, motivated and confident in my ability to achieve the goals I have set, and with gratitude I am open to and welcome the blessings they will bring into my life. I view my self-image with love and acceptance. I am filled with calm confidence and a joyful spirit.*

Free Will and Karma

"True freedom consists in doing things in accordance with right judgement, and not from the compulsion of habits."
Paramhansa Yogananda.
The Wisdom of Yogananda, Volume 7 – 'How to Awaken Your True Potential' (2015), Crystal Clarity Publishers, Nevada City, California.

Will is the ability to make conscious choice. It is the freedom of choice over your action. As a human being, you are endowed with the faculty of choice, of *free will*. Everyone has free will to make their own choices, even if those choices are to obey the commands of others, or to make right or wrong choices. Plants have no will, and animals only have some degree of will, they are free to act, but they are not free enough not to act. In the animal, there is external consciousness with a certain degree of internal consciousness such as being aware of hunger and thirst, but the animal does not have self-consciousness. Their freedom is within the limits of their instinct, which in effect means they are governed by the Cosmic Will because it is the Cosmic Will which determines instinct. *Free will* is only developed in the human beings who are more self-conscious and evolved to be able to think, to reason, to form a conclusion or judgment, and make informed choices. Human free will has its freedom within the limits of intellect, and this freedom that we call *free will* also has its boundaries because the intellect and its process of development is also ultimately determined by the Cosmic Will.

To be able to do whatever you please is not the real meaning of freedom. To have free will and freedom means to act by the power and intelligence of the inner Self, not by the compulsions of desires, moods and habits. You have to choose intelligently. You have no choice but to choose, therefore examine the various choices available to you and choose intelligently and wisely.

Paramhansa Yogananda said, *"You cannot be free unless you have burned the seeds of past actions (saṁskāra and karma) in the fire of wisdom and meditation."* Your past karma influences your present life. Every action you do creates a *saṁskāra* (a subtle latent impression in the subconscious mind of past actions). The *saṁskāra* causes a tendency, which develops into a habit by repetition of the actions. The habit manifests as character, which develops into destiny. In other words, the various actions that you did in the past, your likes and dislikes, and the experiences that you had in the past, shape and guide what you are going to do today and tomorrow.

Your essential nature is *freedom*; you are the master of your own destiny. You need not be a slave of your desires and emotions. Through the power of your own *will*, you can eradicate old habits, negative attitudes and wrong mental impressions. With your *will* you can draw power, courage and strength from within to gradually discipline your mind, and develop new, healthy habits and develop a pure character. The average person has very little *free will* because he or she does not exercise it. In contrast, the enlightened being is one who has gained mastery over his or her own mind, who is always at peace no matter what changes may be taking place in the surrounding world. Such a being experiences emotions but does not become the emotion or become emotional. Constant meditation on your true nature – the unchanging, blissful nature of the true Self – is the key to the power and knowledge within you. When this power and knowledge is revealed, the darkness of ignorance will be dispelled by the light of the knowledge of the Self.

It is the freedom of the self that gives you freedom to choose at the mental level. This freedom is called *free will*. You have freedom of choice or free will over your action, but you have to decide what is right and wrong or proper and improper in your interaction with the world in terms of any action. This is why it is essential for a human being to know very early in life, what is right and what is wrong, what is appropriate and what is not, in any given situation. Once you perform an action, the results are controlled by the natural or cosmic laws. A number of laws, including the law of *karma*, are involved in determining the nature of the result. Sometimes the law of *karma* works in your favour and sometimes against.

If you want to have *freedom* from pain and suffering, rest in your true nature, the blissful Self, the source and support for this life. Through regular daily meditation, you will gain new strength and an inner life of peace, happiness and perennial joy.

We are constantly avoiding all things that are disagreeable to us and pursuing all things agreeable. Most of the endless dissatisfaction many of us experience can be traced to our excessive preoccupation with our body, our senses and our expectation of how the world should be. To have freedom and true happiness, learn to not identify with your body (realm of perceptions and actions), your mind (realm of emotions) and your intellect (realm of thoughts and ideas), but to know them as part of the non-self, as material external to life. Identify with the changeless Consciousness behind these changing forms – the all-pervading Reality supporting them all.

'Won't power'

"*If you haven't enough will power, try developing 'won't power'*," said Yogananda. His advice was that when temptation comes you first have to stop the action or the force. Then when the temptation has gone, you must *reason*, otherwise temptation will overcome all reason. This is '*won't power*' – you just say firmly and with conviction '*No*' and get up and go. Then as the mind gets stronger it yields vision, equanimity, courage, endurance, steadiness, cheerfulness and other blessed qualities.

How to Develop Will Power

In order to create the circumstances to enable something to happen or be done in the development of the will, the following allies will help you:

Attention

There can be no concentration without *interest* and *attention*. Interest develops attention. We all know that it is difficult to focus the mind on an uninteresting object or an object in which we have no interest at all. Our minds have not been trained to endure prolonged attention. The mind becomes bored with monotony and wants to run towards a pleasing and interesting object.

Attention is of two kinds, voluntary and involuntary. When we direct our attention towards an object by determined effort of the will, it is called voluntary attention. Involuntary attention is when there is no effort of the will. We see a beautiful sunset or a beautiful object and our attention is naturally and spontaneously drawn to it.

Attention is the focusing of consciousness. It is the focusing of awareness upon a single object or idea to the exclusion of all else. Simple attention to our lack of awareness is the awakening of awareness.

Through attention, you can attain a profound knowledge of objects. When you listen or look, you receive fully because the attention is steady. When you perceive, there is steadiness, so you take in more things; when you listen, you are steady, so you take in more things.

Your consciousness needs to remain aware and give its full attention to all things, and to whatever you are doing throughout the whole day. This will train your mind and lead to your concentration becoming effortless. Your mind will then become one-pointed instead of scattered aimlessly in all directions. If you do something with your full attention, you will increase your awareness and ability to perform what is right in your thoughts, speech and actions, so that you do not create unrest in your mind.

Concentration

The practice of concentration is of a great help in strengthening the will. By having an intelligent understanding of the habits of your mind – how it wanders, becomes restless and how it operates – you will be able to master your mind. Concentration is essentially freeing the mind's attention from distractions and calmly focusing the full attention of the mind to the exclusion of anything else on any thought that you may be interested in.

The difficulty in understanding the term 'concentration' in the yogic sense is that, commonly, concentration is associated with effort and tenseness. One concentrates in order to defend, possess or achieve something. In this sense, concentration is ego-motivated; it is an outward effort of the will, charged with the energy of the feelings, instead of a calm, steady, *effortless* flow of attention and will power. So in concentration, the less effort is the better. However small or seemingly unimportant, perform all your activities calmly with one hundred percent concentration.

Even-minded calmness
"Be calmly active and actively calm."
Paramhansa Yogananda

If your mind is very restless and scattered, continually moving and unable to be quiet, the energy within you becomes dispersed and very limited in function and in power. The mind in this limited function only reveals to you the material reality, not the infinite possibilities of the spiritual reality. It is only when the mind is absolutely quiet and unified, and in the subtlest state, that your true inner reality – your own spiritual God-Self – becomes revealed to you.

Restlessness is caused by desires. Whatever you do in life, particularly if it takes the form of *desire* – a strong desire for or to do something – it leaves a deep impression on the mind, whether the desire has been satisfied or not. Like seeds planted in the soil of the ground waiting for the right time to be activated to sprout into plants, desire impressions lie dormant in the subconscious mind, creating a tremendous urge within you, making your mind restless.

If the desires are not satisfied, then you become frustrated which can lead to the harmful effects of anger, jealousy, envy and even hatred.

Restlessness can also take the form of emotional excitement, which can bring too much energy through the nervous system and bring an unbalance and hyper-activity to the person experiencing it.

To quieten mental restlessness and emotional excitement, harmonise your thoughts and desires with the inner peace of the Self within you and remain in even minded calmness. Focusing your attention within through daily meditation will bring your mind to a state of active calmness and stillness. In that deep peace, all restless waves of thoughts and sensations will disappear from your mind.

One-pointedness
One-pointedness of mind is absolutely essential if you are to be successful in anything. With the power of concentration, you can focus its rays and make the mind steady. Have a consistency of purpose and concentration of all efforts towards achieving your goal.

Constantly and steadily, be interested in spiritual knowledge, Self-realisation, and the immortal Self within. Always keep in mind your spiritual goal of liberation by reflecting, contemplating, meditating and engaging your total being in understanding the purpose and aim of your life, and aspire to it with enthusiasm, willingness, energy and joy. Seek to transcend your own duality and sense of separation from your Divine Source. Focusing on the highest level of consciousness is a completely conscious choice you must make moment by moment, day by day. Choose to live in the experience of inner freedom, peace, joy and unconditional love.

Using time wisely

If you want to become magnetic and develop a dynamic will, you will need to utilise every second of your time to the best possible advantage, and cultivate your mental, moral and spiritual qualities. Application and tenacity, interest and attention, patience and perseverance, faith and self-reliance will give you a dynamic personality and the inner strength to overcome all difficulties, and to radiate peace and joy to others.

Endurance and Forbearance

The power of endurance is developed by austerity. It is an invaluable quality that strengthens the mind to overcome the obstacles on the spiritual path. Even when at times you may feel very tired and depleted, the power of endurance will give you strength to keep going on.

Endurance requires forbearance – patient self-control, restraint and tolerance. To endure all kinds of difficulties without rebellion or complaint is forbearance.

Forbearance gives you the inner strength, even-mindedness and willingness to continue on the path and not become disheartened.

This forbearance and willingness give you energy, bringing with it great enthusiasm for life, and it removes the negative energies that compel you to do wrong actions.

Contentment – overcoming of aversion, dislikes and irritation

In this world, you will find difficulties and disadvantages everywhere, so if you want to be happy and content never complain against your surroundings and environments. Wherever you are placed, know that you are there to learn something from life and to grow. Therefore, make the best use of every place and situation. Try to live happily and content in any place, under any condition. And if you do fail, see failure as a learning curve and part of life – how boring would a game be if you knew you were going to win every time.

The mind deludes you at every step and every moment. Let nothing upset your mind; overcome the obstacles, difficulties and challenges by cultivating inner contentment. This will give you an inner strength and dynamic personality to conquer any difficulty.

True contentment is the key to the door of spiritual happiness and true happiness is a direct knowledge of the nature of the Self.

Even-mindedness

Maintain constant even-mindedness towards desired and undesired circumstances. This is maintaining equanimity, mental calmness in all situations – in difficult situations, in success and in failure. It is accepting both the good and the bad with equanimity.

Courage in suffering or adversity

Courage contains the qualities of strength, acceptance of life, gratitude, kindness, hope and love.

Courage is not just an act of bravery during a crisis, such as a fireman saving someone from a fire, or a soldier's act of bravery in war. Courage is not defined by what you do, but what you overcome within yourself. It is not the outer victory but the inner victory that counts. Courage acknowledges that life is full of difficulties ordeals and challenges, but also shows that they can be overcome. It brings an inner victory by helping us to overcome our fear, anxiety and resistance to such difficulties and challenges that we have to face in life.

Courage gives you the motivation to act on what you care about, and develops the determination to do it, and carrying it through despite all obstacles. Courage reminds you that life is something precious and marvellous, and it is often when you are challenged that you feel most happy and alive.

Austerity (*tapasyā*)

In Sanskrit, *tapas* from *tapasyā* means 'heat' – the fire that burns up the impurities of the mind and body.

Austerity develops will power and endurance. For meditators, austerity includes accepting whatever happens as the best thing for your spiritual practice, and not being disturbed by any inner or outer discomforts that you may experience.

Patience, restraint and tolerance

Be patient with others; restrain harmful words and actions that may cause suffering to others. Listen with patience and tolerance to those who want your attention, even though they may not be very interesting or charming to you. Patient listening develops the will and wins the heart of others.

Self-discipline

Discipline is essential for success in all fields of life. At the social level, we all practise the external discipline of following national or state laws, social norms, and work ethics. At the individual level, we have internal discipline, which we choose to discipline ourselves. Self-discipline gives you the power to successively attain your goals in life – it gives you patience, endurance, perseverance, restraint and self-control.

Discipline allows you to go beyond limitations to break through boundaries to reach the highest goal. The whole purpose of discipline is to become established in the awareness of the Divine within you. Discipline gives total freedom. The senses of perception are gateways to the Divine, to know the Truth. When the activity of the senses are properly trained and disciplined – refined, sharpened and purified – they can help you to discriminate between what is merely pleasurable and what is beneficial, and to cultivate inner freedom so that you may live fully in the awareness of the Divine, in that light of Consciousness that is within you.

Effort

Effort and self-discipline work together. To discipline yourself is absolutely essential for attaining success in your spiritual effort. Without discipline you will not be able to accomplish the purpose of life.

Make tan earnest effort now! Be very vigilant. Do not allow your sensory desires, habits and environment to control you. From today, determine that you will begin to discipline yourself. You no need to be too rigid and strict with yourself, just start with changing the small things in your life and daily routines: "I will go to bed at 10 p.m. and rise at 6.00 a.m." Discipline yourself to those times, so it becomes a part of your daily routine every day. Once you have decided to do something, willingly persevere with fortitude and fervour, and do not give up. Be determined to succeed. In this way, gradually add more disciplines. Discipline your body, discipline your mind and discipline your speech, so that the soul qualities and virtues hidden within you can be revealed. Be determined to break through the boundaries and limitations that hold you back from divine fulfilment. Self-realisation comes through strong effort; a true seeker is one who never slackens in their efforts.

If you find it difficult to remain resolute, firm and steady on the path of Yoga and spirituality, re-dedicate and inspire yourself now to the Yogic principles and apply self-discipline, with a willing, enthusiastic and aspiring seeking spirit. Then self-discipline will give you inner strength, confidence and satisfaction, that will allow you to lead your life with purpose, awareness, love, respect and freedom. Then you will recognise the disciplines as a source of inner joy and freedom. Remember, whatever kind of effort you put forth now will determine your future destiny. For Self-realisation, effort is more important than destiny.

Right attitude

Spiritual development and the higher practices of meditation are possible only for a totally integrated inner personality. This includes our attitude towards our relationship with life and others. We have to cultivate right and positive attitudes. Actions done with the right attitude increase our vitality, whereas actions done with the wrong attitude dissipate energy. The action itself is neither good nor bad. It is the attitude with which we do an action, the intention behind it, that matters. So whatever your task is, do it with *willingness*, *enthusiasm*, and *joy*, then you will find that you have the *energy* to carry out the task.

Affirm: *"With an attitude of willingness, I discern my next steps. I enthusiastically move forward in faith, ready for the good that I know is unfolding before me. My mind and heart are open to Divine blessings; I willingly step outside my comfort zone, so that my personal development and spiritual growth can expand to new and fulfilling heights."*

The practices of Yoga and meditation cannot yield spiritual realisation of your divine nature without first developing basic moral and ethical virtues. The spiritual seeker who adheres to basic standards of right conduct and attitudes makes spiritual progress.

We do not need another person to show us right conduct, for right conduct is a function of conscience, the inner voice, of the true Self within you. You know when you are doing wrong, because your conscience tells you, and you feel it. The spiritual seeker who has progressed spiritually has the right attitude to life and towards others. Remaining calmly centred within the true nature of the inner Self, the spiritual seeker remains cheerful, optimistic, positive and enthusiastic. He or she does not give in to negative moods, brooding or sulking, gossiping, judging others harshly, and is not provoked to become irritated, angry or resentful. Such a spiritual seeker is not proud or egotistic, he or she adheres to truth, love, spiritual duty (*dharma*), peace, non-violence and goodness (*sattvic* qualities), and shows respect and consideration for others in thought, word and deed. It is the observance of these noble qualities that makes us truly human and potentially Self-realised.

Do the actions and tasks that seem uninteresting to you. This will develop your will, because those actions that are not interesting will become interesting after some time when you have developed the right mental attitude towards them.

Enthusiasm

"Enthusiasm is a volcano on whose top never grows the grass of hesitation."
Kahlil Gibran

The word enthusiasm originates from the Greek *enthousiasmos*. Its roots *en* means 'in' or 'within', and *theos* means God. Enthusiasm literally means 'filled with the energy of God'. Such joyful enthusiasm is the full intensity of emotions and feelings of bliss that comes from the present moment of feeling inspiration.

When you have great enthusiasm, you have rapturous intensity of feeling, enjoyment and passionate eagerness in any pursuit; you have more energy and aliveness. When you feel divinely inspired that truth is on your side – you feel *awake and ready* to achieve great and wonderful things.

Enthusiasm and *energy* go hand-in-hand together. When you are sparkling with enthusiasm, there is a greater flow of energy and vigour in you. It creates a feeling of wonder, inspiration and fresh new ideas in you for moving positively forward. Enthusiasm helps in giving purpose and meaning to life. With enthusiasm, you have the inner power and energy to overcome obstacles and challenges in your life. Enthusiasm or zeal also gives you a lively and keen interest, eagerness, and a great energy in pursuit of a cause or an objective.

You cannot accomplish anything without using your will. Enthusiasm helps in awakening your will, for whenever you are enthusiastic about something, instantly you have the will power to do it. When you lack enthusiasm, there is no will power.

The highest enthusiasm is to experience that Supreme Bliss that we call God or Self. The Cosmos – whole boundless expanse of galaxies – is created and held together by *Divine Will*. Our solar system is only one amongst a vast number of others, and our sun is no more than a star like others; an infinitesimal speck in a vast Galaxy – all this is held together by Divine Will.

People with enthusiasm bring warmth, joy and feeling to their relationships, and vigour and freshness to their activities. Those who are full of enthusiasm inspires others. Such people as Paramhansa Yogananda (1893–1952) and his direct disciple Swami Kriyananda (1926–2013) of the Kriya Yoga path were excellent living examples of being filled with *enthusiasm*. They both gave themselves with joyful enthusiasm completely to God, by which their lives were guided with complete spiritual purpose and God's grace. All those who came into contact with them were filled with light and joy and spiritually inspired. Yogananda and Kriyananda both carried their enthusiasm and strong intention with focused effort, with the right attitudes into every action from morning till night. Their enthusiasm was maintained by a sense of wonder and gratitude with love for everything and everyone around them. They respected life in all its forms. With this joyful enthusiasm and the divine inspiration, inner spiritual power and energy it gave, they overcame the everyday obstacles and challenges of life and attained their spiritual goal of freedom, inner peace and ever-new joy in God.

Enthusiasm – A good prescription for lethargy and apathy

Enthusiasm is invigorating, it is a good prescription for lethargy, fatigue, lack of energy, lack of wonder. Enthusiasm counterbalances boredom and apathy.

Enthusiasm is contagious; if your spirits are low surround yourself with enthusiastic and optimistic people – those who are positive, joyful and enthusiastic, will uplift you. Enthusiasm cannot survive in a negative environment, so be positive in your thinking and attitudes.

Create powerful enthusiasm in your life

• **Be calmly active and actively calm.** To be filled with enthusiasm you do not need to be agitated and excited. As Yogananda said, "*Be calmly active and actively calm.*" In the calm stillness of your peaceful Being, you can still enjoy enthusiasm.

• **Be patient for enthusiasm to endure.** And if you have patience your enthusiasm will be lasting – a lasting and joyful enthusiasm from when you awake in the morning to when you go to sleep at night is what is needed. An enthusiasm that does not wane even when your life is faced with obstacles and challenges.

• **Love what you do, and enthusiasm will naturally follow**. Be grateful for all that you have. Be inspired, be creative and have a passion for what you are doing.

• **Live each moment of your life in wonder and awe** at the incredible beauty within this world and vast universe. Spend time in nature – listen to the sound of singing birds, the sound of rustling leaves in the wind, watch a beautiful sunset. Visit museums to admire the beautiful paintings and sculptures, listen to spiritually uplifting music and read inspiring books by authors that you admire. These are wonderful ways to absorb your attention and generate enthusiasm in you.

• **Develop a positive attitude.** See the positive in any situation. You may not be able to change your external circumstances, but you can change your thinking. Once you can see something positive then use that as a starting point to change your perspective to a more positive one in which you can ignite enthusiasm.

• **Increase your energy.** It takes energy to be enthusiastic. It is difficult to generate enthusiasm when you are tired. Practising Yogananda's *Energisation Exercises* daily, is an excellent way to keep both your enthusiasm and energy high. Also, make sure you are getting enough sleep and that you have a balanced healthy diet and lifestyle to support your spiritual practice.

• **Be discerning with your information intake.** Your enthusiasm and energy can be drained by negative and apathetic voices from people around you or from the media.

• **Create a plan to fill you with enthusiasm.** If you try to achieve a goal without a plan, you will be less motivated and lose enthusiasm.

• **Give your full attention to what you are doing**. Whatever you are doing, give your best and do it well with your full attention and concentration.

• **Set small goals for yourself and begin to achieve them.** The small achievements will help to generate the enthusiasm to continue to greater goals.

Filled with joyful enthusiasm, feel Divine energy and power are flowing in and through you. Feel that energy flow through all your actions. Think and act with joyful enthusiasm knowing that God is within you and that all actions that you perform are offerings to that Divinity within you – the inner Self. With joyful enthusiasm coursing through your entire body express your heart-felt gratitude and appreciation to the Divine within you and see the Consciousness of God within all beings. In this way, you will become a beacon of light giving happiness and joy to everyone around you.

Will Power and Capacity

An important point in developing dynamic will power is to *apply your will according to your capacity*; otherwise, you will become discouraged. Plan your tasks – programme of work or daily routine – according to your capacity. Start your programme or routine with something small, some task that is within your capacity. If you take on too much, or too big a task that is beyond your capacity, your interest will slowly wane, your enthusiasm will gradually decline, and your energy will be scattered and dissipated. Once you have decided to start your task be determined to carry it out and accomplish it without fail. With right feeling and right thinking, focus your will and whole heart with deep attention on the task, then be patient and give it time.

If you accomplish this, you will have taken a small step towards developing a dynamic will power.

Make a list of the things in life that you thought you could not accomplish or set a goal. Then without hesitation put your will into action. If you hesitate, you may lose the opportunity through thinking too much about it, causing confusion and procrastination. Once you set your mind to do something – *Do it now!*

Using your will power focus with deep attention upon accomplishing one thing at a time – *convert your thoughts into will power and will into action.* Each time you accomplish a task or goal see that as a victory for your will power.

Recharging Your Body with Cosmic Energy

The universe, including the human being, is surrounded and permeated by *Consciousness* that is ever-conscious, ever-present, infinite and eternal, and by *Cosmic Energy (Prāṇa)*, the primal, direct, subtle link between Matter and Consciousness, that is structuring and sustaining all things. As human beings, we are indirectly sustained by the food we eat, the water we drink, the oxygen we breathe, and by sunlight. It is written in the Bible, when Jesus said: "*Man shall not live on bread alone, but on every word that proceedeth from the mouth of God*" (Luke 4:4). Meaning that our bodies are not sustained solely by food, water, air and sunlight, but primarily by the cosmic life energy flowing from the Cosmic Source into the body through the subtle centre of the medulla oblongata – *the mouth of God* – that acts as the energy receiver of cosmic energy. This is this flow of cosmic energy that truly sustains us, which Jesus was referring to when he said *every word*.

The cosmic energy that surrounds and permeates the body, enters through the medulla oblongata, located in the brain stem, anterior to (in front of) the cerebellum. This is a cone-shaped, neuronal (nerve cell) mass in the hindbrain, which controls a number of autonomic (involuntary) functions, such as heart rate, breathing, blood vessel dilation, digestion and reflexes like sneezing, swallowing and vomiting. The medulla oblongata also connects the higher levels of the brain to the spinal cord. From the medulla, the cosmic energy then flows to the rest of the body throughout the network of *prāṇic* subtle channels or *nāḍīs*.

Sleep and Energy

During the state of sleep, the life energy (*prāṇa*) withdraws inwardly from the senses and concentrates in the medulla oblongata, where it attracts cosmic energy into the body to sustain and revitalise it whilst the physical body passively sleeps to be recharged and rejuvenated. When you sleep well (both quantity and quality are important) you wake up feeling refreshed and alert, leaving your body and mind rejuvenated for your daily activities.

Deep sleep – A clue to understanding your own *real* nature

"The soul's nature is Bliss – a lasting inner state
of ever-new, ever-changing joy, which eternally
entertains without changing the one entertained
even when he passes through the trials
of physical suffering or death."
Paramhansa Yogananda.
'Yogoda Lessons, Super Advanced Course Number 1 Lessons 1 to 12' (Public Domain).

After a hard day's work, you feel quite exhausted or perhaps unhappy. But after a night's deep sleep, you can say, "I slept well." You feel refreshed and rejuvenated to start a new day. This shows that deep sleep brings us a sense of happiness and peace with it. This is a clue to understanding your own *real* nature. In deep sleep there is an absence of all mental activity, you do not know anything objective, the ego is not present, and there is no conception of time. In sleep your knowledge, and time and space disappear. Your individuality disappears, but you, as Consciousness does not disappear. You, the inner Self, which *is Consciousness, pure Happiness* or *Joy* and *Peace* itself, are all alone there shining within. You have no knowledge of yourself in that deep sleep state, so you can never know that, when you *are* that. Happiness is experienced in deep sleep, but you only become aware of that experience when you return to the waking state. Experience is always beyond the mind. You, or the personal 'I' knows it only when the 'I' comes to that realm of the mind.

In the dream state, time is created by you, whereas in deep sleep you are not aware of time or space. You do not know where you are or have any concept of time. Whatever is created in your dreams is born of your own knowledge, you cannot create something that is totally unknown. *Consciousness* is not bound by or subject to any limitation of time or space.

71

Consciousness being subjective, whole and limitless is always *now*, in the present moment. Everything else is an object of consciousness.

Deep sleep can be utilised directly for establishing yourself in your real nature. To get to your true essential nature, that is ever-existing, ever-conscious, ever-new bliss (*sat-cit-ānanda*), there has to be relaxation of the mind from all forms of activity, whilst simultaneously remaining aware of the happiness and peace experienced in deep sleep. So, just before you sleep and as soon as you awake from sleep, empty your mind of all intruding thoughts and keep your mind absorbed and established only in the thought of your real divine nature, and know that everything other than your real nature (the Self, the Ultimate Reality) is a dream.

Purify Your Thoughts Before You Sleep

One way of purifying your thoughts during the night before you go to sleep is to mentally repeat the mantra *Hong-Sau* until you fall asleep. Lie in your bed in the classical Yoga relaxation pose (*śavasana*) with your arms slightly away from the sides of your body, relaxed palms facing up. Let your feet fall loosely to the sides and remain completely still. Close your eyes and relax your whole body. Maintain the inner focus of your mind by being aware of the natural rhythm of your breathing. Then, focus your attention calmly at the midpoint between the eyebrows on the forehead at the spiritual eye. Imagine the breath flowing in and out at that point. As your breath naturally flows in mentally repeat the mantra '*Hong*', and as you naturally breathe out repeat the mantra '*Sau*' (pronounced 'saw'). By repeating this mantra, you still restless thoughts, withdraw the mind from the senses and calm the mind and life force (*prāṇa*) in the body. You also affirm your real identity as the inner Self. You affirm that the individual self is one with the Infinite Spirit.

**Awareness of your spiritual identity throughout
your daily activities**
*"A wise person is not involved with things that overly
stimulate the senses. Constantly spiritually awake,
filled with the bliss of ultimate Reality, such a one is
peaceful and awakens to the highest realisation."*
Swami Sri Yukteswar (1855–1936)

If you are not alert and aware, habitual thought patterns will dominate your mental field and drive your choices. You will be controlled and limited by your unconscious habits and desires. If you remain aware and centred in your inner Self, thoughts that do not contribute to your inner peace and joy or are inconsistent with your awareness of being can be changed.

Throughout your daily activities, try to remain aware that you are the *changeless* 'I'-principle, the divine Self, that transcends the body, senses and mind, knowing that the activities of the mind – perception, thought and feeling – are constantly changing every moment. Transcending the mind there is only the 'I'-principle, the Self or *Consciousness* that stands alone witnessing all the activities.

Watch your thoughts and cultivate the highest understanding of your own divine nature. Constantly affirm: *'I am Consciousness, I am Bliss, I am the Self'*. *So'ham* (I am That)*, Anando'ham* (I am Bliss) *Sivo'ham* (I am Shiva, the all-pervasive, Supreme Reality). Remember, God, the Supreme Consciousness dwells within you *as* you. That Divine Power, that unlimited Source of energy, that Divine Presence, exists *within* you. It is always available in every moment to you if you wish to connect to it. To allow that Power and Presence to be revealed, you must open up to receive it.

Sleep – A perfect model of death

Sleep is a perfect model for explaining death for the process is very similar. We die every night in sleep. It is almost like a preparation for death. In deep sleep, the sense organs enter into the mind, and the Self withdraws into the subtle body. In death, the soul abandons its physical sheath and is carried within the inner subtle and causal bodies. In sleep, there is only sleep, not even 'I' who sleeps. You do not even know, 'I am asleep.' That is there is no experiencer independent of the experience. There is no ego – (*ahaṁkāra*) is absent in deep sleep, and it is only partially manifest in the dream state. When there is no dream, no thought, nothing – no world – that is complete deep sleep. The world disappears in relation to you and you are not conscious of any phenomena around you. All the persons and all the possessions, power and ego to which you are attached vanish and are forgotten in the state of deep sleep.

At night, as you begin to fall asleep, you initially move into the hypnagogic state, where you start to relax, and alpha waves become predominant in the brain. This is the state of quiet reverie, where many images and memories flash before the mind. As you continue to fall asleep, you move into the deep sleep zone characterised by delta waves and further relaxation. In the next stage of sleep, the dream state, there is a deeper state of relaxation with rapid eye movement (REM), and this is characterised by higher frequency alpha waves. The process of waking follows in the reverse order from REM sleep to deep sleep through the hypnagogic state to complete wakefulness. In Yoga and Vedanta philosophy, these states are known as:

Jāgrat (waking state) – conscious mind, beta waves.
Svapna (dream state) – subconscious mind, alpha and theta waves.
Suṣupti (deep sleep state) – unconscious mind, delta waves.

Beyond these three states is *Turīya*, transcendental, superconsciousness.

In sleep or death, we do not cease to exist, though all objective, individual experience has vanished. In sleep, the mind and its thoughts and mental modifications assume a subtle state. Awareness becomes disengaged from the physical and mental realm of existence.

Dissolution of the body is no more than sleep. Just as a person sleeps and wakes up, so are death and birth. Death is like sleep. Birth is like waking up. The domain of sleep is partly the same domain as the transition into death. In both cases, you enter the subtle astral plane, but in death, depending upon the circumstances, it is generally done with more conscious awareness.

Sleep – overall health and longevity

For optimum health, well-being, and longevity one should sleep for 7–8 hours a night. This should be a top priority in your life. Of course, there are those enlightened yogis – such as Paramhansa Yogananda, who only needed three or four hours of sleep – who regularly meditate long and deeply and draw their supply of energy directly from the Cosmic Source.

If you have insufficient sleep, your body does not have time to complete all the phases needed for muscle repair, memory consolidation and release of hormones regulating growth and appetite, causing you to wake up less prepared to concentrate, and to make decisions. Insufficient sleep produces a tendency to sleep against one's will, and too much sleep dulls the mind and nervous system to such an extent that one is unable to concentrate on the joy of the inner Self. In the *Bhagavad Gita (6:16)*, Krishna strongly encourages Arjuna to lead a balanced life of eating and sleeping for spiritual progress: *"Yoga is not for him who eats too much or who fasts too much, who sleeps too much or who sleeps too little."*

Bedtime Routine
• Keep regular hours for waking and sleeping
Your natural sleep-wake cycle works best when you keep to regular hours, waking at the same time every day, even on the weekend. Trying to catch up with sleep on the weekend can have a reverse effect and make you feel more tired come Monday. Aim to wake to natural sunlight if possible, as this helps to regulate your melatonin levels and keep your sleep cycle on track.

• Avoid Caffeine and energy drinks late in the day
Limit coffee, caffeinated tea, sugary and energy drinks to a combined maximum of two or three a day, and none after 4 p.m., as it takes around six to eight hours for caffeine to leave your system, making it difficult to get off to sleep, shortening your overall sleep time, and reducing the quality and depth of your sleep.

• Eat lightly in the evening
Also, eat lightly in the evening for the digestive firepower is low then. Avoid heavy foods within three hours of bedtime. Avoid spicy or acidic foods, for they can cause stomach problems and heartburn.

• Exercise three to four hours before bedtime

If you do any exercise in the evening, make sure it is done at least three to four hours before bedtime and no later otherwise your body will not be able to relax and return to a calm state in time. Exercises such as simple yoga postures that stretch and relax the body and mind can be practised in the evening to help promote sleep.

• Reduce your fluid intake in the late evening

Drinking large amounts of fluid before bed can disrupt your sleep causing you to get up a number of times in the night to urinate. So, try not to drink any fluids 1–2 hours before going to bed.

• Getting in sync with your body's natural sleep-wake cycle

Getting in sync with your body's natural sleep-wake cycle, or circadian rhythm, is one of the most important strategies for sleeping better. Natural sunlight or bright light during the day helps keep your circadian rhythm healthy. This improves daytime energy, as well as night-time sleep quality and duration. Normally, our energy flows in 60- to 90-minute cycles and the cycle before you go to bed is crucial to how you will sleep. If in the evening in the hours running, up to bedtime you are watching television or using your electronic/technological devices (computer, laptop, tablet, smartphone) the blue light emitted from them will give your brain a rush of dopamine, suppressing your sleep hormones (melatonin), keeping you alert and unable to switch off. So one to two hours before bed have a complete electronic shutdown – no television and no surfing, emails or texts.

• Quiet and calm your mind ready for sleep

During the day, many of us over-stress our brains by constantly interrupting tasks to check our phones, emails, or social media. Try to set aside specific times for these things and focus on one thing at a time.

Remember also, that thinking about not sleeping only keeps you awake. Break the cycle by getting out of bed and distracting yourself, only returning to bed when you are feeling drowsy.

At night give your brain, mind and eyes a rest, forget the world and release all your mental and emotional burdens to God for a restful night. Allow your nervous system to rest and turn within to abide in your eternal nature beyond the body, mind and senses. Ending your day with meditation and a prayer is a wonderful way to let go of stress and worry and find inner peace before falling asleep. Yoga relaxation techniques (deep breathing, visualisation, positive affirmations) help to improve sleep quality. Meditate and pray with gratitude, love and devotion before you go to bed. Evening prayer helps you to see all the good things that happened in your day that you have to be thankful for.

In meditation, the body is still, the senses and the mind turns inward away from all distractions, stimulation and restlessness. When the mind turns inward, it becomes a vehicle to travel back to the source of stillness, beyond the body-mind-senses, to the inner Self.

The *Hong-Sau* Technique (see page 111) is good for calming the mind.

• Make your bedroom environment a sanctuary

To maintain your sleepy state before bed, keep your bedroom as a sanctuary for sleep – dark, comfortable and quiet, with a temperature of around 70°F (20°C), although this may depend on your preferences and what you are used to. Make sure you have a comfortable mattress and pillow. It is recommended that you upgrade your mattress at least every 5–8 years.

At bedtime, you can also spray or place one or two drops of relaxing lavender or jasmine essential oil on your pillow to promote relaxation before sleep.

People who exercise regularly sleep better at night and feel less sleepy during the day. The more vigorously you exercise, the more powerful the sleep benefits. But even light exercise, such as brisk walking for 15 minutes a day, can improve sleep quality.

Sleep rejuvenates and revives your vitality, but during the day when you work or study or are involved in a tiring activity, you may find that your energy becomes depleted. It is during those times when your energy is feeling low that Yogananda's *Energisation Exercises* become very useful in recharging your body battery, by drawing a supply of cosmic energy at any time and whenever needed, from the ether by the power of *will*. Within 15 minutes of enthusiastically practising the *Energisation Exercises* you will be renewed and vitalised.

The Energisation Exercises

Purpose of the Energisation Exercises

*"The whole purpose of true exercise is to
awaken the inner source of energy which
we have ignored throughout our lives."*
Paramhansa Yogananda.

*"The Energisation Exercises teach how to recharge the body battery
with fresh life current by increasing the power of will. They strengthen and
recharge the muscles with vital force, not only collectively but individually,
and teach how to surround each body cell with a ring of super-charged
electrical vital energy and thus keep them free from decay or bacterial
invasion. They keep not only the muscles, but all the tissues of the body,
bones, marrow, brain, and cells in perfect health, and cause the
resurrection of dying tissue cells and worn out faculties, and the formation
of billions of new cells."* – Paramhansa Yogananda.

The primary purpose of the *Energisation Exercises* is to learn to awaken and
direct the flow of energy (*prāna,* life force) throughout your body. By
controlling your energy, you can gain mastery over the subtle energy (*prāna*) in
your body.

Prāna (Life force)

Prāna is the universal all-permeating force of Nature which vibrates
through all life and is the vital link between the gross and the subtle world.

Prāna is the energy that pervades the entire physical system that acts as a
medium between the body and the mind. The manifested universe is composed
of *Prāna* (Energy). *Prāna* is more subtle than the physical body but grosser
than the mind. *Prāna* acts but does not think; the mind is more subtle.

Although we cannot see *prāna,* its existence can be inferred by the process
of our breathing, for air is drawn in and out of the lungs by the action of *prāna.*
In reality, this vital energy we call *prāna* is one energy, but appears to be more
than one when viewed from the standpoint of its different functions.

Prāna is known as *vayu,* or 'vital air', when it operates within the human
body systems. In both the subtle and the gross bodies, *prāna* has been
differentiated into five major and five minor *prānas,* the only difference being
that of subtle and gross according to the bodies. Disturbance of the *prāna* in the
body is the primary cause of many mental and physical diseases. That is why

the practice of *prāṇāyāma* is important for maintaining this balance. The daily practice of the *Energisation Exercises* also help in maintaining that balance by consciously drawing Life Energy (*prāṇa*) into the body. By using maximum use of conscious Will and Life Energy (*prāṇa*), you not only exercise and vitalise the muscles, but all the tissues and cells of the body. This requires your conscious Will and concentration on the Life Energy within you to awaken the consciousness of your spiritual nature. Then you realise that your strength comes from within and not from your muscles, and that life does not solely depend on food or exercise but is sustained by the Life Energy (*prāṇa*) that is within you.

When the subtle body permeates the gross body, the subtle *prāṇas*, like the gross ones, are also present in the subtle body. Without *prāṇa*, no activity can take place in the subtle body, nor any support of life. Subtle *prāṇa* performs all actions in every part of the body. After death of the physical body, it is the *prāṇa* that sustains and takes the subtle body to the astral plane.

Benefits of the Energisation Exercises

Regular practice of Yogananda's *Energisation Exercises* promotes both mental and physical relaxation. They develop dynamic will power, by means of using the *will*, with *awareness* of energy, to consciously draw energy into your body, and direct the flow of energy to specific body parts. The circulation, digestion and respiration and nerve function are all benefited by the practice of the *Energisation Exercises*. Through the use of conscious breathing, directing the life force (*prāṇa*) and concentrated attention, the techniques of the *Energisation Exercises* enable you to draw abundant energy consciously into your body, strengthening and purifying all the cells and tissues of the body systematically in turn.

Benefits:

- Tones and strengthens the muscles and tissues of the body.
- Increases lymph and blood circulation.
- Oxygenates the blood through proper respiration.
- Increases general vitality and energy.
- Abdominal muscles and digestive system are harmonised and invigorated.
- The spinal adjustment exercises stretch the spine, relieving undue pressure on the nerves issuing from between the vertebra.
- Reduces stress, nervous tension, anxiety, and hypertension.
- Eliminates fatigue and tiredness.
- Memory and brainpower are increased.
- Prepares the mind and body for meditation.

The two most important things for bringing the energy in the mind and body under control are: *awareness* and *will power.* These *Energisation*

Exercises are a means of using conscious will power with awareness, to consciously draw this cosmic energy (life force, *prāṇa*) the infinite potential of God within you, into the body cells and, afterward, to withdraw it again from the body in meditation. The mind cannot act directly upon the body. It must act through a medium of energy. The *will* first acts upon the energy, then the *energy* acts upon the body. Developing a deep inner flow of energy is important to our experience of spiritual awakening because like a flowing river it washes away all the debris – the obstacles and blockages that keep us bound to body consciousness, and our separation from the Divine Consciousness. By expanding the flow of energy within, you have greater access to freedom and inner joy.

Yogananda's *Energisation Exercises* give awareness of the energy, and that awareness gives the ability to manipulate its flow in the body at will. We incorporate that awareness into our disciplined inner practice by establishing a flow of energy within. This is how we come to experience spiritual energy moving through our body. It is this divine Cosmic Energy, that is a communicating link between the mind and body which truly sustains those who serve with *willingness* and with *awareness* of Divine Presence.

When you practise these *Energization Exercises*, do them with the *will*, the power of God within you. Usually when we use the word will, we think of tension in an effortful way, so use the word, *willingness*. **The greater the willingness, the greater the flow of energy.** Yogananda defined **will as desire plus energy, directed toward fulfilment.** In other words, it is something you should enthusiastically want to do. In that way, practise these *Energisation Exercises* **with willingness, with the desire that your body be filled with energy and joy!** The positive will centre in the body is the spiritual eye, at the point between the eyebrows. By strong concentration at this point, will power can be exerted to draw a limitless flow of energy through the medulla oblongata.

Concentrate on the Flow of Energy

As you do the movements with a *calm inward awareness*, be conscious of the energy flowing through a subtle portal located at the medulla oblongata, inside the brain stem at the base of the skull. Then by using your will power concentrate *on the flow of energy* to the specific body part or centre of the particular muscle group, and consciously direct the flow of energy to it. You can try visualising the flow of limitless energy as a stream of light, coursing through your body to the various parts you are directing it to.

From a gradual increasing flowing rhythm – low, to medium, to high tension, to the point where it vibrates, hold the tension for a few moments, consciously filling that body part with energy. Then exhale and slowly relax in the reverse order, in a decreasing flowing rhythm from high, to medium, to low, and completely relax, *feeling* the energy as it withdraws from the body part. Be consciously and aware of the energy *inwardly* behind that tension and vibration. The more aware you are of the energy, the greater will be your control over it. Always **tense with will; relax and feel**.

At first, what you will feel is just the physical tension inside the muscles. Then you will experience the flow of energy which creates the tension in those muscles. Finally, you will become aware of how you can direct the flow of energy to them. As you practice, you can mentally repeat: **"The greater the will, the greater the flow of energy!"**

Learning to direct energy has a practical benefit because we can apply these principles on mental and spiritual levels as well. The more aware you are of the flow of energy, the more you can direct that energy by will power or willingness, not only to the body, but to anything that you do – towards self-improvement, service toward others, toward your work, toward creative inspiration, toward the Divinity within you in meditation. In fact, when you are attuned with this energy it can be harnessed and used in all aspects of your life to transform it.

Guidelines for Practising the Energisation Exercises:

1. **Practise the exercises with willingness, enthusiasm and joy**! When you have willingness, and are happy and positive, you will experience an increase in energy. And the more you become *aware* of using your willingness to *direct* that energy, the more you will be able to increase the flow.

    Remember Yogananda's maxim: **"The greater the will, the greater the flow of energy."**

2. **Contract and relax the muscle group gradually in a continuous wave from low, to medium, to high tension, vibrating with great will power – 'Tense with will; relax and feel'.** Hold the tension for three or four seconds, but do not tense so hard that you cause physical discomfort, or soreness. After tensing, relax gradually, in a smooth progression from high, to medium, to low, and completely relax and feel the flow of energy suffusing the area which has been energised. If you find it difficult to isolate a muscle or body part, concentrate and focus your mind there and the energy and *prāṇa* will automatically flow to that part – *energy follows thought. The greater the will the greater the flow of energy!* Use your willingness to align your will with the greater Source of Energy that is all around you.

3. **Many of the exercises are practised with a double breath.** Double breathing helps to oxygenate and detoxify the blood. It is practised with a short, sharp inhalation through the nose followed directly by a longer, smoother inhalation, completely filling your lungs. Then, without pause, exhaling through the mouth and nose with the same double breath (Ha-haaa).

4. **Modify or leave out exercise if necessary.** There should be no pain or discomfort associated with them. If you were ill or had neck, spinal, or any other physical disabilities, you can practise the exercises with low tension or visualising the energy flowing in a current of light to the affected body part, as you mentally do the exercise.

5. **Feel that through the power of your will, you are consciously drawing and directing a limitless current of energy or light force into your body.** After tensing a body area with will, completely relax and feel the results. Conscious relaxation after each exercise is very important; tensing and relaxing not only recharges the body cells with energy, but more importantly, trains you to bring the flow of *prāṇic* energy under conscious control. As you practise the *Energization Exercises* keep this affirmation in your mind:
   "My will is attuned to Divine Will, the unlimited and Infinite Source of all power and accomplishment."

6. **Feel that through the power of your will, you are consciously drawing and directing a limitless current of cosmic energy or light force into your body.** After tensing a body area with will, completely relax and feel the results. Conscious relaxation after each exercise is very important. Tensing and relaxing not only recharges the body cells with energy, but more importantly, trains you to bring the flow of *prāṇic* energy under control. As you practise the *Energization Exercises* keep this affirmation in your mind: *"My will is attuned to Divine Will, the unlimited and Infinite Source of all power and accomplishment."*

7. **Practise the *Energisation Exercises* daily** in the morning and evening, preferably outdoors, or if indoors then with a window open so that you can oxygenate your lungs with fresh air and draw *prāṇa* into them. Each of the exercises are practised from three to five times. When you have learned all 39 exercises in the correct sequence of practising them, it will take you no longer than 15 minutes to do them. Practise them before meditating to release mental and physical tensions. This will then allow you to go deeper into the stillness of meditation. These exercise can also be practised at anytime and anywhere, and because they are all performed from a standing position you need very little space to practise them in. If you have less time, then it is suggested that you just practise the 20-part recharging exercise (step 20 of the 39 *Energisation Exercises*). After having learned and memorised the practice of the *Energisation Exercises*, you can practise them with your eyes closed or half closed, with your gaze directed to the point between the eyebrows, the centre of spiritual perception and will power. This

will help you to interiorise your consciousness and keep your mind in superconscious.

Cautions

If you suffer from high blood pressure, it is advised that you use medium rather than high tension during practice of the exercises. If you have an injured muscle, then apply only light tension when sending energy to a muscle or group of muscles. If you are unable to tense the muscle at all, then send energy to it only mentally. If you have a condition which prevents you from practising any of the *Energisation Exercises* through physical movement, then do it mentally, even if you have to sit on a chair or lie down. Remember, *energy follows thought*, so you can still direct energy to anywhere in your body through conscious will and awareness.

Practice of the 39 Energisation Exercises

The following 39 *Energisation Exercises,* a unique system devised by Paramhansa Yogananda for consciously drawing Cosmic Energy into the body, are best learned from a teacher who can guide you through them correctly. It will be much quicker to learn the exercises from a teacher then trying to follow them from a book. If you cannot find a teacher then the next best way is to obtain a guided video or a guided audio CD, which can be obtained online (see resources at back of book).

Begin by standing upright with your hand folded in prayer at your chest and pray:

"O Infinite Spirit, recharge this body with Thy cosmic energy, and conscious vitality. Recharge this mind with Thy deep concentration, clarity and determination. Recharge this soul with Thy ever-new joy. O eternal youth of body and mind, abide in me forever and ever. Aum, Amen."

1. Double Breathing (with Palms Touching)

Begin the *Energisation Exercises* from the standing position, with your arms extended out to the side at shoulder level, and with a double breath exhale, bringing your arms together in front of you, with your palms touching, and your knees bent. With a double inhalation, tense your entire body upwards in a wave, as you straighten your legs and pull your arms back outward against a resisting force. Then, with a double exhalation relax downward in a wave through your body, bringing the arms together again and bending the knees. Repeat 3 to 5 times.

2. Calf Recharging and 3. Ankle Rotation

Balance on your right leg, with your left knee slightly bent. Then slowly pull your left leg upward, bending at the knee, whilst tensing your calf muscle, as if you are pulling your leg up against a resisting weight. Relax briefly, and then push the leg down against a resisting weight.

Practise 3 to 5 times, and then lifting your left foot a few inches from the floor, lightly tense your ankle and rotate it in small circles 3 to 5 times in each direction.
Repeat with the other leg.

4. Calf and Forearm; Thigh and Upper Arm

Stand with the weight on your right leg, and place your left leg slightly in front, and simultaneously tense your left calf muscle and left forearm gradually from low, to medium, to high tension, and then vibrate them. Relax the muscles gradually in reverse order – from high, to medium, to low, then completely *relax and feel the energy.*

Repeat this with your thigh and upper arm muscles. Alternating between the upper and lower muscles, do this three times on the left side, then three times on the right.

Then with your weight equally balanced on both legs, tense both calves and both forearms simultaneously, and relax; and then both thighs and both upper arms and relax. Repeat 3 to 5 times.

5. Chest and Buttock Recharging

Simultaneously and gradually, tense your left buttock and left chest from low to medium, to high tension, and vibrate with energy. Then gradually relax them and repeat on your right side. In this way, alternate from the left side to the right 3 to 5 times.

6. Back Recharging

Tense and relax the lower back muscles, in the lumbar area, alternating left and right 3 to 5 times.

Then, tense and relax the middle back muscles, between the shoulder blades.

Finally, tense and relax the upper back muscles, above your shoulder blades.

7. Shoulder Rotation

Rest your fingers on your shoulder blades and rotate the shoulders with tension in large circles 3 to 5 times in each direction.

8. Throat Recharging

Tense and relax your entire throat and neck muscles 3 to 5 times, and then alternating, tense and relax the left side of your neck, followed by your right side 3 to 5 times.

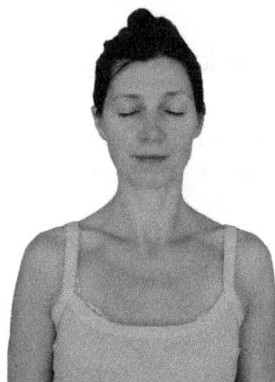

9. Neck Recharging

With a double exhalation, slowly lower your head until your chin is close to your chest. Then, as if your chin were tied to the chest, and with a double inhalation, pull your head slowly up and back, vibrating the neck muscles. Relax slowly downwards with a double exhalation and repeat 3 to 5 times.

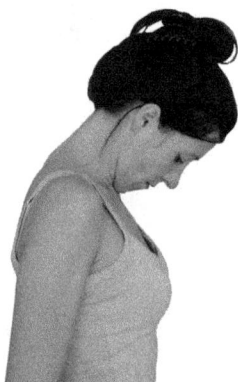

10. Neck Rotation

Tensing the muscles on the inside and outside of your neck, rotate your head three times in one direction, and then in the other direction. Repeat the rotations without tension.

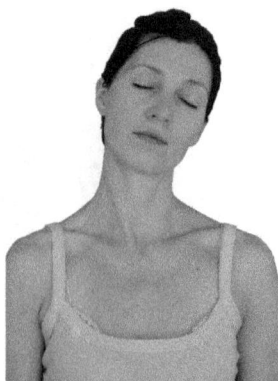

11. Spinal Recharging (Lower Spinal Adjustment)

Stand with your feet hip width apart, with your arms bent at the elbow and placed at the level of your hips. Twist your hips and lower body to the right whilst simultaneously moving your shoulders to the left. Alternate the twisting to the left and to the right several times with brisk, defined movements.

12. Spinal Rotation and 13. Lateral Spinal Stretching

Stand with your feet hip width apart with your hands on your waist. Then with your head aligned with the spine and looking straight ahead, bend slightly forward arching your spine. With tension in the arched spine, rotate your trunk 3 to 5 times in each direction, while keeping your hips and legs still.

Stand with your feet hip width apart with your hands on your hips, and with tension in your spine, push against the tension to the left, and then to the right, several times.

14. Vertebrae Adjustment

Bend slightly forward with your fists pressing firmly on the muscles on each side of your spinal column. Starting at the base of the spine, and pressing inward and upward with your knuckles, arch your spine and thrust your upper body backward, while coming up onto your toes. Repeat this movement with the knuckles positioned one vertebra higher with each cycle.

15. Upper Spinal Adjustment

Stand with your feet hip width apart with your arms straight out in front of your body at the level of the shoulders. Keeping your hips and legs still, draw your arms back to the left with tension, bringing your right hand to the chest. The head and eyes simultaneously follows the motion of the outstretched arms. Relax back to the starting point and repeat to the right side. Practise 3 to 5 times, alternating to the left and right sides.

16. Brain Cell Recharging

Briskly and gently, rap your entire skull and forehead with your knuckles to stimulate the energy in the brain cells. Visualise your brain cells being awakened with Cosmic Energy.

17. Scalp Massage

Press your fingertips firmly on your scalp and move the scalp forwards and backwards, left and right, and then rotate in each direction. Then move your fingers to another position on the head and repeat until your entire scalp has been massaged.

18. Medulla Memory Exercise

Joining together your forefinger, middle finger and ring finger of each hand, position them at the medulla oblongata (the hollow at the back of the neck where it meets the skull), and with pressure there rotate them in small circles in each direction several times. Then bring your head slowly back against the pressure of your fingers as you take a double inhalation. Feel the energy entering through the medulla oblongata, then with a double exhalation, relax the tension and bring your chin down to the chest with a firm but not too strong movement. Repeat 3 to 5 times.

19. Biceps Recharging

Clasp your hands above your head and gradually tense your bicep muscles (low-medium-high), vibrate and then relax. Alternate to the left and right several times.

20. Twenty-Part Body Recharging

Phase one: Stand with your feet hip width apart with your arms down by your sides. With a double inhalation, simultaneously and gradually tense all your body muscles (low-medium-high), vibrate the whole body strongly, then relax gradually (high-medium-low) with a double exhalation.

Phase two: Gradually, tense and relax each of the twenty body parts individually, alternating from left to right: starting with the feet, calves, thighs, buttocks, lower and upper abdominal muscles, forearms, upper arms, chest muscles, neck (left side, right side, front and back).

Phase three: Repeat the exercise, this time maintaining the tension at a medium level in each body part, as you slowly inhale, synchronising the inhalation to last until you have completely tensed all the body parts. When the entire body is tense, vibrate it briefly with high tension.

Phase four: Then, relax each muscle individually in the reverse order as you slowly exhale, again synchronising your exhalation to last until you have relaxed down through all the body parts. Begin the relaxation phase by bringing your chin to the chest, relaxing all the muscles in your neck, and continue down the body releasing first the right side and then the left, until you have completely relaxed your whole body. *Relax* and *feel* your body is a dynamo of energy!

Phase five: With your chin still on the chest, take a double inhalation and gradually tense, and vibrate your whole body with energy, and then gradually relax with a double exhalation.

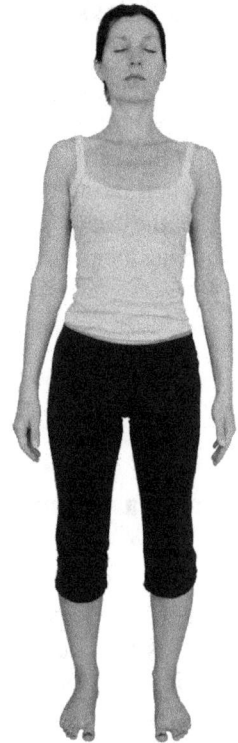

21. Weightlifting in the Front

Stand with your arms down at your sides, with your fists facing each other, and tense your arms as if you are pulling up heavy weights. Vibrating the arms with energy, bring your fists to your chest, relax briefly, and push them down with the fists still facing each other. Repeat several times. Optional: double inhalation with the upward movement and exhalation with the downward movement.

22. Double Breathing with Elbows Touching

With your elbows bent at right angles, raise your arms to the sides of your head at shoulder level. With a double exhalation, bring your elbows together in front of your chest as you bend at the knees. With a double inhalation, vibrate with energy and pull your arms back to the starting position, as you tense the lower body in a wave upwards, similar to the first exercise. Repeat several times.

23. Weight Pulling to the Side

With your arms extended to your sides at shoulder level, and parallel to the floor, clench your fists in an upward position, and draw your arms towards the head, as though pulling heavy weights towards you. Relax briefly and push your arms out again, making them vibrate with energy. Repeat several times. Optional: double breathing.

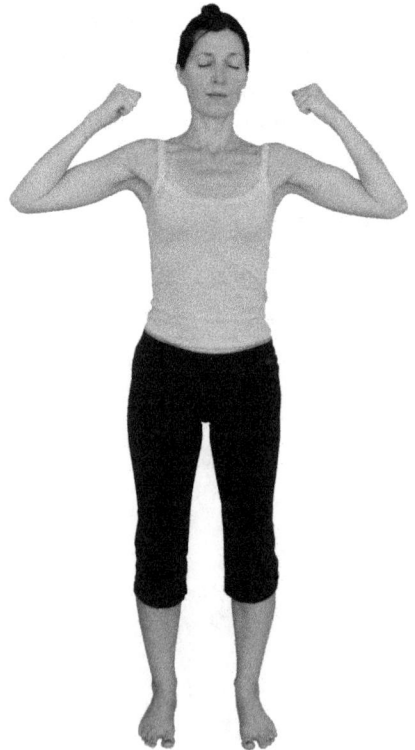

24. Arm Rotations in Small Circles

Stand with your arms extended to your sides at shoulder level with your fists facing upwards, rotate your arms in small circles, tensing strongly all the time. Then relax momentarily and rotate in the opposite direction.

25. Weight Pulling to the Front

Position your arms bent at right angles in front of you, so that the backs of your fists are close to your forehead. Then extend your arms straight out in front, vibrating them with energy, as though pushing weights. Relax briefly and pull the weights back in towards your head. Optional: double breathing.

26. Finger Recharging

Stand with your arms relaxed down at your sides, open and close your hands vigorously several times with tension. Repeat the exercise with your arms extended laterally, then again with your arms extended at shoulder level in front of your body, and finally with your arms extended straight above your head.

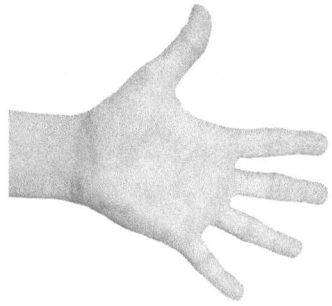

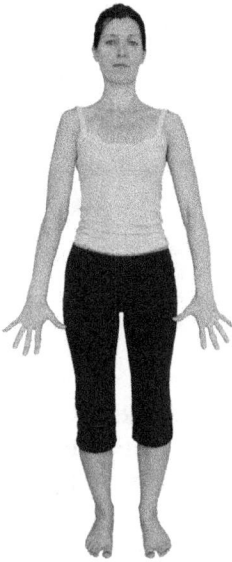

27. Arm Recharging in Four Phases

In the starting position bring your fists up to your chest.

a. While inhaling with a **single breath**, push your arms out to your sides with tension in the arm muscles, relax briefly, and then pull them back with tension to the starting position and relax briefly.

b. With tension again in the arms, and a **single exhalation**, push the arms out in front of you, relax briefly, and pull them back with tension to the starting position.

c. Now with tension and a **double inhalation**, lift them over your head, while rising up onto your toes.

d. With relaxed arms and a **double exhalation**, bring the weights down to your chest, and then down to your sides, as you come down off your toes.

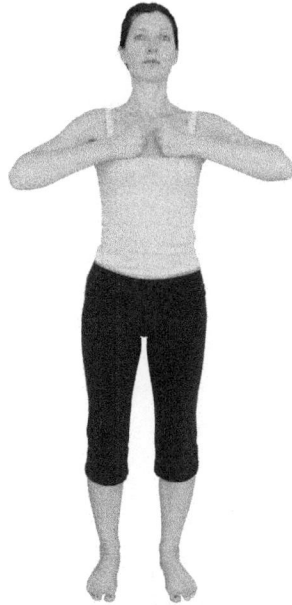

95

28. Overhead Weightlifting (Single Arm Raising)

Tense your left arm as though you are holding a weight in your hand, and inhale with a double breath as you lift it over your head, coming up onto your toes. Then with a double exhalation, relax your arm as you bring it back down. Repeat with alternate arms several times.

29. Lateral Weightlifting

With your feet hip width apart, tense your left arm as though holding a weight, and with a double inhalation bring your arms up laterally until the upper arm touches your head, bending very slightly to the right side. With a double exhalation relax your arm downwards and repeat with alternate arms several times.

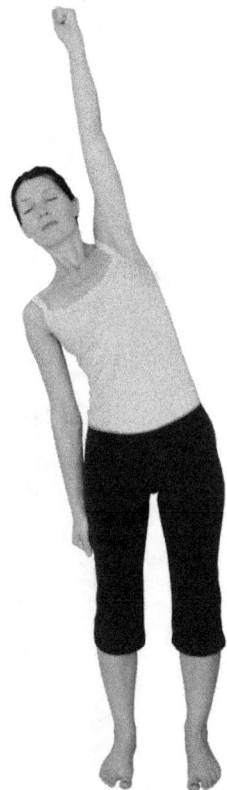

30. Walking in Place

Walk in place with an exaggerated marching step, lifting your knees high and swinging the opposite arm to the opposite leg. Continue for 50 to 100 steps, remaining aware of the energy flowing to and through your body.

31. Running in Place

Run in place, lifting your knees as before, and at the same time bring the heels up to touch your buttocks if you can. The arms remain stationary, bent at the elbows. Practise 50 to 100 steps, being aware of the flow of energy to ad through your body.

32. Fencing

With both fists on your chest, step forward with your left leg and, with a double exhalation, thrust your right arm and fist to the front, as though you are pushing a very heavy door. Keep your spine straight and tense, with tension as well in the chest, the back leg and the extended arm, as you move from the standing to the thrusting position. Both feet are flat on the floor. With a double inhalation, relax and return to the standing position, and repeat the exercise with the other leg and arm, alternating several times.

33. Arm Rotation in Large Circles

Inhaling, lift your tensed arms in a large arc over your head, and with an exhalation bring them down behind you, relaxing them. Repeat at least three times in each direction.

34. Abdomen Recharging

First phase: known as *uddiyana bandha*. Exhale completely, as you bring your upper body forward, resting the heels of your hands on the thighs. With the breath still held out, contract the abdominal muscles as far as possible inward and upward towards the spine, and hold for as long as comfortable, without strain. Slowly relax the abdomen, then inhale, and return to the upright position.

Second phase: The second phase is known as *agnisar kriya.* Exhale again and resume the forward position resting the palms of your hands on the thighs. This time contract and expand the abdominal muscles repeatedly, for as long as you are able to retain the breath externally. Relax, inhale and return to the upright position. This is a very good exercise for awakening energy in the navel centre or *manipura chakra.* As well as stimulating the digestion and toning the abdominal organs and glands.

Third phase: Abdominal rolling (*Lauliki Nauli*). Bend your knees again and lean forward, pressing your hands on your thighs just above the knees, and keeping your arms straight. Exhale deeply, and firmly contract your abdominal muscles, bringing the navel toward the spine. This is *uddiyana bandha.*
Maintaining this lock, press your hands into your legs and give a forward and slightly downward thrust to the abdominal portion between the navel and pubic bone.

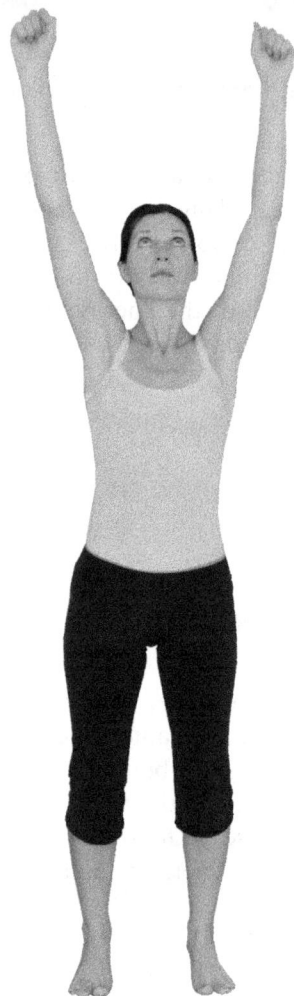

This helps to contract the rectus abdominis muscles – the two long vertical rows of muscle running down the centre of the abdomen – keeping the other muscles of the abdomen in a relaxed condition. Equal hand pressure on your legs helps you to achieve the isolation of the rectus abdomens muscles. Once you can achieve this initial isolation of these muscles, try to isolate just the right rectus muscle (*Dakshina Nauli*) by leaning your body forward, tilting your torso slightly to the right and putting extra pressure on the right hand. Then try to isolate the left rectus muscle (*Vama Nauli*) by leaning slightly to the left while increasing pressure on the left hand. Finally, start trying to move each one from side to side so they move or 'roll' in a wave-like movement in quick succession. Begin by doing this five rolls to the right and five to the left.

Note: It will take time and perseverance to master abdominal rolling; as it is an advanced exercise that requires voluntary control of the abdominal muscles. You will need to learn how to isolate, contract and rotate the rectus muscles in a churning motion while maintaining a static posture. This practice is therefore best learned under the expertise of an adept yoga teacher. However, it is included here because, once learned, it is a valuable practice that contributes toward awakening of dormant *kundalini*, helping it ascend through the *sushuma* to the crown chakra.

Caution: Practise only on an empty stomach. Allow three to four hours after a meal before practising. The ideal time to practise is early morning after evacuating the bladder and bowels.

Contra-indications: Women should not practise during pregnancy or menstruation (*agnisar kriya* stimulates the upward flow of *pranic* energy, which is counter to the natural downward cleansing flow*)*. Those suffering from high blood pressure, heart disease or acute peptic, duodenal ulcers, or hiatal hernia should not practise these stomach exercises, nor should persons who have undergone abdominal surgery in the last six to nine months.

Benefits: *Nauli Kriya* regenerates, invigorates and stimulates the abdominal viscera and the gastrointestinal or alimentary system. *Nauli* improves digestion by stimulating the digestive fire, thereby removing toxins, indigestion and constipation. Tones the abdominal muscles and massages the internal organs. The liver and pancreas are toned.

Uddiyana bandha practised regularly will enable you to exhale more completely and breathe more comfortably and efficiently. *Uddiyana bandha* improves circulation to the abdominal organs because it draws blood from the abdominal cavity into the chest and back to the heart. The decreased pressure in the capillary beds and veins of the abdominal organs facilitate more blood flow through those organs as well as more efficient fluid exchange with their tissues.

35. Double Breathing with Palms Touching

Double-breathing with the palms touching. Stand with your arms straight out to your side at shoulder level, exhale with a double breath. Bend your knees slightly and bring your arms to the front, so that your palms touch. With a double-inhalation, tense the entire body upwards in a wave, as you straighten your legs and pull the arms back outward against a resisting force. With a double-exhalation, relax the body downward in a wave. Repeat 3 to 5 times.

36. Calf Recharging and 37. Ankle Rotation

Balance on your right leg, with your left knee slightly bent. Then slowly pull your left leg upward, bending at the knee, whilst tensing your calf muscle, as if you are pulling your leg up against a resisting weight. Relax briefly, and then push the leg down against a resisting weight.

Practise 3 to 5 times, and then lifting your left foot a few inches from the floor, lightly tense your ankle and rotate it in small circles 3 to 5 times in each direction. Repeat with the other leg.

38. Hip Recharging

Balance with your weight on your right leg
and extend your left leg about a foot forward
with the foot close to the floor and rotate
your foot three or more circles in each
direction. Repeat on the right side.

39. Double Breathing Without Tension

With your mind calmly focused at the point between the eyebrows and looking
inwardly with closed eyes, bring your fists to your upper chest, holding them
forward. With complete relaxation, and a double exhalation, extend your arms
slowly in front of you. Pause and enjoy the flow of energy you feel throughout
your body. With a double inhalation, slowly draw the arms back to your chest,
pausing again to feel the energy flow. Repeat six to 10 times.

With your eyes closed, continue to focus your attention inwardly at the point
between the eyebrows. Feeling relaxed, peaceful and energised, enjoy the
pauses between the breaths, and mentally affirm: *"I am eternal! I am blissful! I
am free!"*

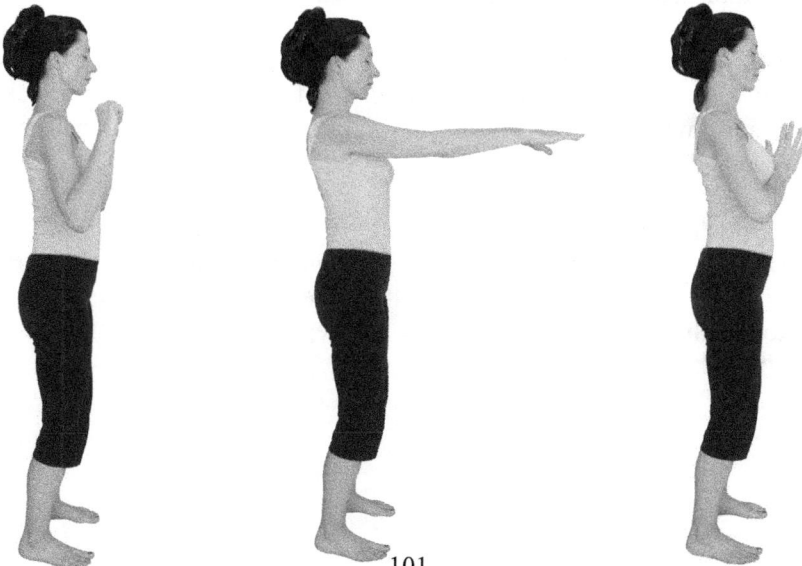

Energisation Exercises (Short Version)

Here is a shorter version for those who are unable to practise the complete version of the 39 *Energisation Exercises*.

1. Double Breathing (with palms touching)
Stand with your arms straight out to your side at shoulder level, exhale with a double breath. Bend your knees slightly and bring your arms to the front, so that your palms touch. With a double-inhalation, tense the entire body upwards in a wave, as you straighten your legs and pull the arms back outward against a resisting force. With a double-exhalation, relax the body downward in a wave. Repeat 3 to 5 times.

2. Shoulder Rotation (with hands on shoulders)
Rest your fingers on your shoulder blades and rotate the shoulders with tension in large circles 3 to 5 times in each direction.

3. Spinal Rotation
Stand with feet hip-width apart with your hands on your waist. Then with your head aligned with the spine and looking straight ahead, bend slightly forward arching your spine. With tension in the arched spine, rotate your trunk three to five times in each direction, whilst keeping your hips and legs still.

4. Upper Spinal Adjustment
Stand with your feet hip-width apart with your arms straight out in front of your body at the level of your shoulders. Keeping your hips and legs still, draw your arms back to the left with tension, bringing your right hand to the chest. The head and eyes simultaneously follow the motion of the outstretched arms. Relax back to the starting position and repeat to the right side. Practise three to five times, alternating to the left and right sides.

5. Brain Cell Recharging
Briskly and gently, rap your entire skull and forehead with your knuckles to stimulate and awaken the energy in the brain cells. Visualise your brain cells being awakened with Cosmic Energy.

6. Scalp Massage
Press your fingertips firmly on your scalp and move the scalp forwards and backwards, left and right, and then rotate in each direction. Then move your fingers to another position on the head and repeat until your entire scalp has been massaged.

Twenty-Part Body Recharging

Phase one: Stand with your feet hip width apart with your arms down by your sides. With a double inhalation, simultaneously and gradually tense all your body muscles (low-medium-high), vibrate the whole body strongly, then relax gradually (high-medium-low) with a double exhalation.

Phase two: Gradually, tense and relax each of the twenty body parts individually, alternating from left to right: starting with the feet, calves, thighs, buttocks, lower and upper abdominal muscles, forearms, upper arms, chest muscles, neck (left side, right side, front and back).

Phase three: Repeat the exercise, this time maintaining the tension at a medium level in each body part, as you slowly inhale, synchronising the inhalation to last until you have completely tensed all the body parts. When the entire body is tense, vibrate it briefly with high tension.

Phase four: Then, relax each muscle individually in the reverse order as you slowly exhale, again synchronising your exhalation to last until you have relaxed down through all the body parts. Begin the relaxation phase by bringing your chin to the chest, relaxing all the muscles in your neck, and continue down the body releasing first the right side and then the left, until you have completely relaxed your whole body. *Relax* and *feel* your body is a dynamo of energy!

Phase five: With your chin still on the chest, take a double inhalation and gradually tense, and vibrate your whole body with energy and then gradually relax with a double exhalation.

Whole-Body Breathing
Stand erect, with the feet hip-width apart and feet parallel (*Tadasana*). Then with a complete exhalation through the mouth, bend your trunk forward from the hips and relax your arms, neck and back into a standing forward bend (bend your knees slightly to avoid strain). Then slowly raise your upper body whilst inhaling through the nose, bringing your arms forward and up, and tensing them as though lifting a heavy weight. Tense your body in an upward-moving wave as you come upright and into a slight backward bend with medium to high tension. Practise 3 to 5 times.

Caution: Persons with high blood pressure, heart disease or glaucoma should not practise this exercise

Swami Kriyananda's
Superconscious Living Exercises
(For Generating Positive Enthusiasm and Energy)

During the thirty years I followed Swami Kriyananda (who initiated me into the ancient science of Kriya Yoga in London 1983), from his teachings I found the *Superconscious Living Exercises* to be very practical and useful for generating my positive enthusiasm and energy. These exercises complement Yogananda's *Energisation Exercises* very well.

The *Superconscious Living Exercises* – a short sequence of exercises used with positive affirmations is performed from a standing position, and is simple, quick, and joyful to practice. These six exercises simultaneously use a physical movement with a positive affirmation – the physical movement adds power to the affirmative words, and the affirmations give direction and purpose to the physical movements, adding an inward focus to the practice.

The *Superconscious Living Exercises* effectively produce instant positive enthusiasm, energy and joy!

The exercises can be practised before meditation to clear and focus the mind. They are also beneficial to practise if you are feeling low in mood, tired, depleted or fatigued – to restore and revitalise you, and give you inner strength.

When you are faced with mental obstacles and challenges in your life practise these six *Superconscious Living Exercises* to raise your positive energy. Then meditate using the *Hong-Sau* Technique (see page 127) to connect to your inner Self, and know that during these meditative moments of inner calm and stillness in the silence of your innermost God-Self, that you are never alone, that you are always supported and guided by the One Presence that is unlimited and available to you at any given moment.

Affirmation: *My inner strength is greater than any outer appearance. Wherever I go, whatever I do, I am divinely guided, supported, and protected by the One Presence of the Divine light within me. Guided in right decisions the inner light of spiritual understanding shines through every problem and circumstance, dissolving all obstacles.*

I affirm divine order in every area of my life. Divine love and wisdom illumine and direct my will. Abiding in awareness of my true nature, I am always inspired to be higher purpose-directed. As an immortal spiritual being, I live in freedom and joy! I am healthy, happy, and creatively expressive.

1. Standing in one place, walk vigorously while affirming:

I am awake and ready! I am awake and ready!

2a. Stand erect with your feet together and with your hands in fists held at the centre of the chest, then extend your hands vigorously out to the sides in line with your shoulders while at the same time affirming aloud:

I am positive!

2b. Bring your hands back to the chest, then extend your arms vigorously in front of you while affirming aloud:

Energetic!

2c. Bring your hands back to the chest, the vigorously extend them high above your head while affirming:

Enthusiastic!

2d. Then relax the arms by your sides.

Repeat the exercise three or more times as you feel necessary.

3. Stand erect with your hands formed in relaxed fists, and lightly rap your knuckles along your arms, shoulders, legs and torso, while affirming aloud:

I am master of my body! I am master of myself!

Repeat the exercise three or more times as you feel necessary.

4. Standing in the same position, using the palms of your hands briskly rub your arms, legs, hips, chest, abdomen, and back, while affirming aloud:

Awake!
Rejoice my body cells!

Repeat the exercise three or more times as you feel necessary.

5. Standing in the same position, with relaxed fists, rap your scalp lightly with your knuckles, affirming aloud:

Be glad, my brain.
Be wise and strong!

Repeat the exercise three or more times as you feel necessary.

6. Standing in the same position, using your fingertips, massage lightly your entire scalp, affirming:

Awake, my sleeping children! Wake!

Repeat the exercise three or more times as you feel necessary.

Positive Affirmations and why they work

An affirmation is a positive sentence or phrase that you repeat on a regular basis to make a formal declaration to yourself and the universe of your intention for it to be the truth.

To use a positive affirmation, first, determine what kind of transformation you want to bring about in yourself - a goal or intention. Or determine what quality, attitude, value, or characteristic you want to remind yourself of or develop in yourself.

Regularly throughout the day consciously choose to repeat your positive affirmation. You can repeat it either aloud, softly whispered, or mentally.

If you repeat your affirmation at every opportunity available to you it will begin to replace the negative thinking that takes over when you are not aware of or monitoring your thoughts.

Our minds can be likened to a garden. If the garden is cultivated with the right soil, and planted with useful seeds, and given careful attention, it can flourish and bring forth a healthy abundance of flowers, fruits and vegetables. But if the garden has poor soil it will have poor growth. If the garden is neglected and no useful seeds are planted, then it will only produce useless weeds. Similarly, we need to be mindful of the thoughts we choose to think and speak. If our minds are cultivated with positive, kind, caring, wise, loving, and peaceful thoughts, our minds will become like a beautiful garden. Affirmations are like seeds planted in soil. By consciously choosing positive worded affirmations they will help to transform your thinking and empower you. They can help to eliminate your negative beliefs and negative habitual thinking patterns and help create a more positive life experience.

Some examples of positive affirmations:

"With a grateful mind and heart, I open to divine supply, and feel abundantly blessed."

"I am ready and willing to fulfill my divine potential."

"I embrace life with cheerful optimism. Each moment is filled with unlimited possibilities."

"God's all healing power flows in and through me now."

"God's radiant healing energy flows in and through every cell, tissue, and organ of my body. I am whole and well!"

Empowering Yourself
Your Thoughts Create Your Reality

"Self-disciplined thinking and behaviour will
empower you to be wisely decisive
and constructively intentional."
Roy Eugene Davis (1931-2019), a direct disciple of Paramhansa Yogananda.

If your primary identification is with your body-mind-senses, then your ego-self is the dominant force in your life. For it is the ego, or programmed self, that creates a sense of self and an identity from the thoughts about yourself. The thoughts and beliefs about yourself affect how you feel about yourself, how you experience others, and what kinds of people you attract. Love is your true divine nature; it is only ego-illusory ideas and beliefs that create an obstacle to experiencing your true essential nature. Those beliefs that allows love to flow within you and within those who you are relating to is closer to the truth.

When you are aware of yourself as a spiritual being expressing through a mortal physical body and a subtle mind, you can observe your body-mind witnessing your own existence. You can then be the master of your body-mind-senses, rather than being controlled by them. This gives you empowerment to control your own destiny, for you are the creator and selector of your thoughts.

When you are truly a master of your mind, you empower yourself with wise choices avoiding all thoughts that weaken you – shame, guilt, apathy, self-pity, despair, fear, anger, resentment and hatred – the negative thoughts that keeps you away from your true Source of divine power that is love, peace, harmony, kindness and joy.

Habits are created by repetitions of your thoughts, and it is your habits and thoughts that create your reality and determine how you respond to your daily situations in life. Ego manifests in the limiting habit of thought and behaviour that emerge from your identification with the body-mind, deluding you into forgetting that in truth you are a divine spiritual being that is changeless, ever-conscious, ever-new joy. When a false sense of self-identity is accepted as true, the mind is modified and fragmented, the intellect is clouded, awareness is confined, and powers of perception are limited.

The practice of Yoga meditation constantly reminds you that you are not the limited, non-eternal physical body nor the mind, but the changeless infinite Self. The Self, the still centre of your own being is joy or bliss (ananda) and is ever-new. That bliss arises unconditioned from within, and it can be experienced and understood only when you have attained That.

Meditation awakens the memory of your real divine nature. To be truly alive and empowered is to know your own Self.

To avoid and permanently end all forms of misery and suffering, you have to cultivate a constant awareness of your real spiritual nature through perseverance in acquiring wisdom of the Self and practising Yoga meditation. Make it a practice to meditate regularly and deeply. Then, after meditating, hold on to the divine after-effects of awakened Self-consciousness and its virtues – inner joy, peace, harmony and love – and express them in your daily life.

Fulfilling the Divine Purpose of Life

"The purpose of human life is to find God. That is the only reason for our existence. Job, friends, material interests – these things in themselves mean nothing. They can never provide you with true happiness, for the simple reason that none of them, in itself, is complete.
Only God encompasses everything."
Paramhansa Yogananda

As spiritual beings having human experiences, we are here to discover the magnificent truth of who we are. It is this truth in you that will bring you to the goal.

'You shall know the truth, and the truth
shall set you free.'
The Bible, John 8:32

The purpose of human life is to realise your Divine nature; that God dwells within you *as* you (the Self). It is to realise and become established in the awareness of your true essential nature – the changeless supreme Self – that higher power that exists within you. Until you come to this realisation, no matter how many of your desires are fulfilled, you will never be happy; you will remain discontented and continue to suffer in ignorance of not understanding the mystery of your own existence. There is a feeling of being disconnected, separated, a feeling of something *missing* from your life, an emptiness that cannot be filled by endless desires and their promises of fulfilment. Through not understanding the distinction between pleasure – an attribute of the senses; and happiness – an attribute of the mind, we become restless seeking the delusory charms, pleasures, thrills and temptations of the world. In trying to give meaning and purpose to our lives, we fill it with events, activities, things, people and we create circumstances that will fill our emptiness and discontent.

The happiness that originates outside of yourself, that you invest in things, objects and people, is always elusive and transitory. Your pursuit's in a futile search for happiness is a poor investment; there is no security or fulfilment in it. Your greatest investment is to regain your awareness of your divine nature and discover the reservoir of power *within* you. When your life is an expression of the inner state of joy, you discover and experience true happiness and regain your freedom. The realisation of your true nature, which is attained through meditation, will result in the perfect knowledge that your real Self is immortal, undying and unchanging. When you are deep in meditation you attain unity with your true nature; you are united with your own inner Self, which is *Sat-Cit-Ānanda* – existence, Consciousness and Bliss absolute, or as Yogananda referred to it – *ever-Conscious, ever-Existent, ever-new Bliss.*

Sat means absolute Truth, the Truth that is ever-existing in all places, in all things, and at all times. The Self is not bound or limited by any place, thing or time. Not a single molecule, atom, proton, or even finer or subtle particle is without the presence of God as *Sat*, ever-Existing. God, the Self is omnipresent and present within us.

Cit means ever-Consciousness or Awareness in all existence. God, the Self is omniscient, All-Knowing. It has the power to know, to feel, to experience. That which *knows* is Consciousness and all it ever knows is itself. It does not need a mind or a body to know itself. Consciousness knows itself directly. The mind, the body, the world, and the universe are projected within Consciousness and made only out of Consciousness. Like the candlelight that makes things visible in the dark, Consciousness (*Cit*) reveals whether or not an object exists. It shines through all objects. It is the light of all lights. Consciousness is Self-luminous, Self-Knowing, Self-evident and Self-existent.

The essential nature of our Self, 'I', Knowing-Being, Absolute Awareness, is Consciousness and Presence. In order for Knowing or Consciousness to be present, there must be Being. And so, to experience the presence of our Being, Consciousness must be present.

Ānanda means God, the Self, is ever-new Bliss or Joy. We seek joy in everything because the very nature of the Self is bliss or joy. That joy is inherent in everything in existence. *Ānanda* indicates the inner source of happiness, the true source of fullness and contentment.

All that we see and experience is God – *sat-cit-ānanda*. You are made in the divine image of God; your real nature is identical to that of God, just as the nature of a wave and the ocean are to water. Your essential nature is pure existence, awareness and bliss. You are an eternal, conscious being, which is the true source of happiness. Whenever you say "I", using the first person pronoun, you are ultimately referring to the inner Self. The Self is not a third person – he, she, or it. The Self is the core or the essence of who you are.

The Three Great Blessings in Life:

1) **To be born in a human body**, for it is only in a human body that you can recognise divinity within yourself; that you are an embodiment of supreme Truth; that the *Kingdom of God* is within your own being; that

the highest Truth exists *within* your own being. Your own body is not merely a physical body but a divine temple that embodies and enshrines the innermost sanctuary of the divine Self, which is *Sat-Cit-Ānanda* (Ever-existent, Ever-Conscious, Ever-new Bliss).

2) **To have the desire to know the Truth, God (supreme Consciousness), the Self.**

There comes a point in your life when you feel a strong desire to know the Truth, to know God, to know the great power that exists in all things, to know that there is meaning and a higher purpose to your life than what your ego-mind and environment has conditioned you to accept. It is remembering your real Divine nature, for to forget your own divine Self and consider yourself something else is *ignorance* – the root cause of all sorrow and suffering. The knowledge, awareness and realisation of your own true nature is the source of true happiness, joy, peace and contentment.

3) **To have a true Self-realised Guru who has attained the Truth**, who can lead you from the unreal to the real, from darkness to light, from illusion to Truth, from duality to Unity. The Guru's sole aim is to elevate the disciple to a higher state of consciousness, to awaken the disciple from forgetfulness of his or her true spiritual nature to the light and knowledge of the inner Self. The Guru dispels darkness and bestows light and removes ignorance and instils knowledge of the Self in a Truth-seeker.

It is through the Guru's great wisdom and grace that you can realise the divinity, the omniscience dwelling within your heart and experience divine joy, inner peace and contentment.

The three main purposes toward finding true inner and outer fulfilment in life:

1. **To seek and find true lasting happiness**
2. **To realise your full human potential**
3. **To balance the material and spiritual aspects of your life**

When you have the right understanding that the purpose of all experiences are to stimulate and encourage your spiritual development, then you have the right attitude to life and to meditation.

If you do not know your higher purpose in life, meditation and inner reflection will help to reveal it. Then you will be able to unfold your innate qualities and awaken your inner potential. Paramhansa Yogananda said: *"Focus your attention within. You will experience new power, new strength, and peace in body, mind and spirit. All limitations will be vanquished."*

Our spiritual journey is not always an easy one. Just by choosing to lead a spiritual life, we are swimming against the current, or 'going against the grain'. The world around us is flowing in one direction but we have decided to go in another. Most people in the world are identified with their body, mind and personality characteristics, resulting in a false sense of separation from their true divine nature. By entering the spiritual path of meditation, we have decided to remove this delusive error of perception by having *direct* knowledge of the Truth, Reality, or Self- God; to experience *directly* in meditation what we are as pure existence-being. When you accept this fundamental position that your present state is a state of ignorance (*avidyā*), then it is clear that your true purpose and effort should be given to spiritual life, because spiritual life is the life that is dedicated to the finding of eternal Truth, the ultimate Reality (God), in which we find ultimate fulfilment.

An Introduction to Meditation

"The more you feel peace in meditation,
The closer you are to God."
Paramhansa Yogananda.

The purpose of meditation is to go inward and tune in to that Divine Source *within* you; to discover the deeper Truth and Reality of who you are. To do that you need to let go of everything in life that has reinforced that you are limited and separate from your own Source – the eternal, changeless Divine Self – your true inner Being.

The truth of the Self is not something you have to acquire, or to go in search of – it already *is*. The Truth you are seeking is ever-present with you now. You are the Truth, the Reality; the Consciousness of God is within your Being here and now. The Self, or Consciousness is the very core of your *being*. It does not require any other light, because it is self-luminous. Things depend upon varying proofs to establish their existence, but the 'I' (Consciousness) is self-evident, it is self-luminous (*svayam-prakāsha*), it is the light of lights, it does not require any other light for its manifestation. With my Pure Existence, or Pure Awareness, I know that *I am*. This 'I am' is Existence; the knowing aspect is Consciousness; and the joy derived from this knowledge that 'I am' is the blissful (*ānanda*) aspect of the same Existence.

All effort, including Yoga techniques and meditation, is only to remove the physical and psychological obstacles that stop you from establishing yourself in the Truth.

To experience your real nature of *Sat-Cit-Ānanda* (ever-Existent, ever-Conscious, ever-new Bliss), the real changeless 'I'-principle, you must transcend the body, senses and mind and the objective world. Remove the thought aspect from the 'I'-thought, and what remains is the permanent background to all thoughts – the real '*I*', or '*I am*' – your innermost Self. The thoughts and the world can only shine by your light. The changeless 'I' is the self-luminous principle.

During your daily activities, try to remain Self-aware of that changeless 'I'-principle, whilst knowing that the activities – action, perception, thought and feeling – themselves are changing every moment, and are not part of your real nature.

To transcend your experience of duality to living in a state of Unity, meditate and reconnect with your real essential nature – the divine Self, that is *sat-cit-ānanda* (ever-conscious, ever-existent, ever-new Bliss). Affirm your divine nature: "*I am Pure Consciousness.*" By affirming '*I am Pure*

Consciousness' the 'I' and 'Consciousness' cannot be objectified, therefore this affirming thought or contemplation can never draw you outward away from your centre, it drives away all intruding thoughts and can only take you inward, ultimately merging in the *Consciousness* (the Self).

Your True Nature Is Spiritual

"The true state of the Self, the soul, is bliss
wisdom, love, peace."
Paramhansa Yogananda.

Your true nature is *spiritual*. Its attributes or qualities are: *happiness, peace, love, joy, truth, wisdom* and *power.* These attributes are ever present within you, but due to loss of awareness of their presence within you, you have become identified with your body and all material things related to the body, causing you to experience discontent, desire, attachment, fear, anger, unhappiness and suffering. Meditation helps to free you from this great misunderstanding of false identification by restoring the awareness of your Self, as a spiritual Being, that is ever-existing, ever-conscious, ever-new bliss (*sat-cit-ānanda*). When you actually experience this *directly*, you will know that you *are* that truth, happiness, love, peace and joy that you seek. These eternal attributes are enshrined within you, in the eternal Self. You are innately peaceful, blissful and full of love. The Self appears to be conditioned by virtue of ignorance, but when ignorance is eradicated, the unconditioned Self – that is distinct from both the gross and subtle bodies – shines by its own light, like the sun when the clouds have disappeared. That which shines just before and after every thought and feeling is the "I", the objectless consciousness; that is the Self. It shines as bliss in deep sleep and in deep meditation. The Self is the Light of Consciousness in all thoughts and perceptions and the Light of Love in all feelings. The Self, Consciousness, is the perceiver of the body, breath, prana, and mind-modifications. Those who are forgetful of the Self, one's true nature, mistakenly identify with the body, mind and senses, and consequently live in bondage. What you perceive, sense, experience, think or feel is not who you are. In reality, you are the Light of Consciousness in which perception, sensations, thoughts and feelings come and go; they are transitory and subject to change. To abide in true happiness, peace and joy, and become liberated from bondage, one has to use wise discrimination to rise above this wrong identification.

Meditation is the most effective way to explore and understand the mystery of life – to know who you are – what is your real nature or identity? Why are you here, what is your relationship to life; what or who is God, the ultimate Reality? Meditation is the key to both Self-knowledge and the Self of the Self (God). As the wave takes its existence from the ocean, so we take our being from God. And just as the wave and the ocean are One, so is the individual Self (*ātman*), in essence, eternally one with the Supreme Self (*Paramātman*), the ocean of Conscious Light that is God.

Through Self-awareness, an awakening to who you really are, meditation allows you to return your consciousness to its true essential nature. It is through *direct experience* of meditation that you become more Self-aware and experience your true essential nature as happiness, peace, love and joy. Once you have been awakened to the truth of your own being, you must learn to nurture that experience in every possible way and continue to practice steadfastly for a prolonged period to stabilise what you have attained. When you have attained wisdom of the Truth through enlightenment, ignorance will no longer delude you.

> "Self-realisation is the knowing - in body, mind, and soul – that we are one with the omnipresence of God; that we do not have to pray that it come to us, that we are merely near it at all times, but that God's omnipresence is our omnipresence; that we are just as much a part of Him now as we ever will be. All we have to do is improve our knowing." – Paramhansa Yogananda.

Being aware and present of the Self within you at all times

The effects of sitting for meditation may only last for a short while after your practice. So to sustain the energy, peace, and joy of the meditation effects throughout the day, you will need to remain in the awareness and the presence of the inner Self. This is important if you want to awaken spiritually; to become Self-realised. You need to remain aware of your essential *Beingness*, the 'I Am', the essential identity as Consciousness itself at all times, not only when you sit for meditation, but constantly throughout all activities. Self and God-Realisation is not something that you expect to happen at the end of your life or in the next life, but it is to awaken *here* and *now*! The Truth, the Light of God, Consciousness, is inseparable from who you are, but you have to become aware of that and not be deluded by ignorance. Your actual experience in this moment is undeniably present now and it has no objective qualities. It is only the presence of *Awareness* and *Being*, which together constitute your real or essential nature, the Self.

You may sit to meditate and enter a transcendental state of joy and peace, but then later on as you go through the days activities of work, meeting people, travelling, and so on, you may find that you have forgotten your essential nature, the awareness of your own Presence in the now moment of each moment. And through loss of that awareness and presence of the inner Self, you slip back into your old habits, wants, desires, wrong attitudes, and incessant thinking, ego-reacting to problems and to others. A sense of separation starts with a thought of identifying with your body and ego-personality. Limitations arise. And consequently, you lose the Presence of 'I Am', you lose your inner peace and joy, and Oneness with life.

Our search for happiness, peace, joy, and love is inherent in the belief and feeling that we are separate. We have long forgotten our Oneness with life, and with the Absolute Reality, God. Through meditation and Self-knowledge, we need to return to knowing our own Being, its knowing of itself. To be established in the Self is to realise that God lives in us and we live in God, we are never separate from that Supreme Consciousness.

Remembering Your True Nature

"I am the Self abiding in the hearts of all beings."
- Bhagavad Gita 10.20.

The nature of the Self is *Consciousness, Knowledge, and Bliss*. It can be known only by direct realisation. Realisation and liberation is cessation of bondage (ignorance) and perception of our real or true nature (the Self). To attain direct realisation of one's own Self one needs to regularly and attentively meditate on the divine Self within. That inner divine Self that is unseen and subjective is the only changeless and eternal Reality. Everything else is subject to change and therefore impermanent. Our misperception of our true nature is because we have a body and an ego-mind, and we mistakenly identify with that transient aspect of our existence. In forgetfulness of our Oneness we think "I am different", "I am the doer", "I am separate"; we get lost in duality.

The inner Self, the Knower, the Witness, the Conscious Principle - "I" is distinct from both the physical and the subtle bodies, including the mind.

To change our reality, we need to change our perception and transform our consciousness. We need to discriminate what is real and what is unreal. Discrimination of the real means the determination (the process of establishing exactly) that the nature of the Self is changeless and eternal, whereas all that is perceptible is unreal, because it is subject to change and is impermanent.

Meditation is the means to establish your awareness in the true Self. It is through the power of your own will and attention that you can establish yourself in a more expanded state of consciousness in meditation. By reversing the process of identifying with objects within manifestation, and opening and expanding your awareness, you will discover the Source within you that underlies everything. It is remembering "I am that Conscious Principle in this body, that is Self-knowing".

When there is intention and willingness to learn and to awaken to Self-realisation, progress can be steady and fast. Knowing that you are a spiritual being will empower you to be confident and firm in your resolve to be fully awake to the truth of who and what you are.

How to Remain Aware of the Inner Self

Due to habitual thinking, being overly preoccupied with personal concerns, being too outward directed, letting subconscious inclinations be too influential, and excessive stimulation of the senses, we forget our true nature as a spiritual Being (inner Self). This divine Presence that dwells within you is an eternal, individualised image and likeness of God, the Infinite, Eternal, Conscious Being. It is through the Self within that we know our oneness with God. All the attributes of God - power, love, peace, calmness, happiness, joy or bliss, harmony, and wisdom - are within you, you do not have to search for them externally. The Kingdom of God is *within* you. You are an individual expression of God, the ultimate Reality. You are the divine expressing in human form, you are part of the divine flow and you can never be separate from God, the One Presence, the One Consciousness, the One Love, that permeates all of creation, the Source of all energy. In Oneness, God lives and moves and has expression in each one of us.

Aum (OM)

'Whoever knows OM, the Self, becomes the Self.'

Mandukya Upanishad.

In the Mandukya Upanishad an ancient Vedic text, it says that AUM (OM) stands for the supreme Reality. It is a symbol for what was, what is, and what shall be. AUM represents also what lies beyond past, present, and future.

It is through the Self within that we know our oneness with God. When we try to think of the Absolute, the mind finds it difficult, for it does not have anything tangible to grasp. It seems beyond our grasp; an abstract concept or idea, like the words love, beauty, or truth. We need an image or a symbol to relate to. We need to give the mind some support to hold onto. If you wanted to get someone's attention, you would say that person's name. Similarly, if you want to make contact with Divine Being or God, the name to use is the sacred sound syllable AUM, which when chanted or intoned sounds as OM. Its vibration embodies the Divine Presence. This sacred mantra is repeated to evoke to the mind a sense of that Reality we are seeking to know directly. OM is the *expression* and not just the symbol of God; it is both the Consciousness and the Power that is God. AUM (OM) is mentioned a number of times in the *Bhagavad Gita*: "I am the sacred syllable OM (*Pranava*) in all the Vedas"(*Bhagavad Gita 7.8*). "I am the sacred syllable OM (*Omkara*)"(*Bhagavad Gita 9.17*). "Among words I am the single syllable OM" (*Bhagavad Gita 10.25*).

In the ancient *Yoga Sutras*, the Sage Patanjali says: "Its (the Supreme Being) *expression* is the syllable OM. Constant repetition of that reveals its meaning. Then one attains inner awareness, and obstacles no longer arise" (*Yoga Sutras* 1.27-29).

This is the secret of remembrance of that Divine Presence we call God. From the practice of the constant repetition (*japa*) of OM, its meaning is revealed, transforming your awareness. From that remembering comes the realisation of the divine inner Self and the removal of all obstacles. The practice of constant repetition of OM with awareness, stills the constant chatter of the mind with all its thoughts, feelings, and emotions, so that you abide in your own essential nature, (the unchanging, self-luminous Self; Consciousness) the witness of the mind. Otherwise you will identify with the mind's activities and remain in the ordinary state of ego-self awareness.

"Meditate on OM as the Self"
(*Mandukya Upanishad 2.2.6*).

"One should meditate on this syllable OM. That is the quintessence of the essence, the Supreme, the highest"
(*Chandogya Upanishad 1.1.1, 3*).

"Constant *japa* (repetition) of the *Pranava, Omkar (OM)*, which is self-revealing, and constant focus on it as the form of *Ishwara* (Supreme Lord), and dedicating all actions to it as if you are not the doer yourself, is *Kriya Yoga*."
(Yogiraj Shyama Charan Lahiri Mahasaya).

Practice: Constant repetition of OM

The practice of the constant repetition (*japa*) of OM can be done sitting in meditation, which is easier to do than walking outside where there are many distractions. But it is an excellent practice to do throughout the waking hours of the day when you are moving or walking outside because it will enable you to *abide in the stillness of your inner Being* without the constant distractions and mental activity of the mind. The continual repetition-intonation of the sacred mantra OM will imbue you with the power and consciousness inherent in the mantra.

When you are by yourself and not engaged in conversation, or concentrated on studying or working, mentally intone OM by synchronising it with your natural and spontaneous breathing. So as you inhale mentally intone the O sound of OM, then at the exact moment as the exhalation begins, intone the M sound of OM throughout the exhalation. The OM sound should not make two disconnected sounds of O and M but a prolonged and continuous sounding of OM, so that the O merges with the M sound. Intoning OM in this way with the breath unifies the breath from duality into unity.

As you practise *Om Japa Pranayama* keep your mind relaxed, alert, and aware. If thoughts, subconscious impressions, or inner sensations arise to distract you, then just acknowledge them and calmly release and ignore them. Remaining alert and aware, return to the practice of mentally intoning OM. With practise you will be able to remain in the here and now present moment whether you are sitting or walking. This is of great benefit because you will be able to switch off the constant chattering of the voice in your head that has many stories and dramas, the thought processes, and their reflection in the body as emotion. Even when you are out and about mentally intoning OM, such as walking in a park or in the countryside in Nature, you will still be able to simultaneously keep your mind aware to enjoy your natural surroundings through your senses - the sight of beautiful trees and clouds, the sun's rays dancing on the branches through the leaves to the ground, sounds of birds, the fragrance of plants and flowers, the sensation of the cool or warm air on your skin. There is an aliveness of energy in the body. There is a sense of Oneness with the life around you in which separation dissolves. You are aware of being organically related to the whole universe at every moment. Awareness is all-inclusive attention. It is this simple experience of being aware that remains ever-present and changeless in the background of all experience.

By inwardly listening to the mental intonations of OM you become aware of the divine Self and the Self of the Self, God. This practice will keep you abiding in your innermost Self - existence, consciousness, love - transcending the obstacles and restrictions of the ego-mind. It awakens the memory of who you are in Reality. It takes you to *direct* realisation of the ever-present non-dual love that is the nature of the Self. It is the joy of Being, the joy of being conscious, it is the joy of enabling consciousness to flow into what you do, it is the joy of living in the Presence of God.

Yoga Results from the Stilling of the Mind's Activity

The great ancient sage, Patañjali (third or second century BCE), states in his *Yoga Sutras 1:2–4*, that, "Yoga results from the stilling of the mind's activity, and to experience this is to abide in one's own essential nature (of the changeless, self-luminous Self, the Source and Witness of the thoughts). Otherwise, one falsely identifies with the mind's activities."

It is due to forgetfulness of your real identity, your true being as self-aware consciousness that you falsely identify with the mental activity and the transient worldly forms, which become the source of all your woes, sorrow and unhappiness.

Then, in *Yoga Sutra* 1:12, Patañjali teaches us how to still the mind's activities: "The stilling of the mind's activities arises through continuous practice (*abhāsya*) and dispassion (*vairāgya*)."

What Patañjali is referring to here is that to still the mind's activities one needs to practice (*abhāsya*), to make an uninterrupted, persistent, and disciplined effort toward steadiness in the awareness of the Self for a long time. This requires the exercise of one's will, but it needs to be balanced with dispassion (*vairāgya*), non-attachment and freedom from desire. Together, practice and dispassion are like the two wings of a bird – to fly a bird needs two wings. Similarly, to make spiritual progress and advance toward Self- and God-realisation, both *abhāsya* and *vairāgya* are absolutely essential.

Further on in the *Yoga Sutras*, Patañjali, introduces the 'Eight Limbs of Yoga' (2:29–55; 3:1–3) – moral precepts (*yamas* and *niyamas*), posture (*asana*), life force control (*pranayama*), withdrawal of the senses (*pratyahara*), concentration (*dharana*), meditation (*dhyana*) and absorption (*samadhi*). I have covered these in great depth in my book, '*The Supreme Art and Science of Raja and Kriya Yoga*', and also in a clear and more concise form in my book '*Yoga Meditation*', I recommend both books for further study.

Investigate Your True Nature and Meditate to Experience It

Examining and understanding the nature of your mind and higher realities, and the regular practice of meditating superconsciously on a daily basis is important and necessary for recognising your true spiritual identity and rediscovering your innate spiritual qualities – *happiness, peace, love, joy, wisdom* and *power* – the very substance of your conscious existence, your very own Self. Meditation along with Self-inquiry into your true nature behind your mind and personality helps you to find peace in understanding, to discover the path to true knowledge of the Self, and to master your own mind and its mental activity. With mastery of the mind you are able to eliminate the obstacles to Self- and God-realisation, by eliminating negative and disturbing thoughts, bad habits and wrong attitudes, and restore a positive inner environment by generating a flow of positive thoughts.

In meditation, you remove your awareness from your physical body and senses and turn your attention inward to reconnect with the spiritual Self. For the beginner this can be quite a challenge. There are two main obstacles to overcome. The first obstacle is the physical body that needs to sit in a comfortable and steady posture without movement for a length of time. The second obstacle is the mind, which is unseen, subtle and can move very quickly. The mind is difficult to control and quieten, for the mind can be very restless with incessant and roaming thoughts, making it very difficult to focus the attention and to concentrate on one point of concentration. So, the first step in learning to meditate is to relax both the body and the mind and to free them from all distractions.

Practising the *Energisation Exercises* Prior to Meditation

It takes discipline, effort and *will power* to sit perfectly still, in a comfortable, steady and relaxed position. It also takes *energy* and *calm focused concentration* to overcome the restless nature of the thinking mind, to meditate deeply.

Practising the *Energisation Exercises* prior to meditation effectively help in entering a calm, interiorised state of awareness. The *Energisation Exercises* release all nervous tension and stress from the body, but they also recharge the body with cosmic energy – they awaken the energy in the spine and brain.

Guidelines for Meditation Practice

Setting the Intention

Decide now and positively resolve to make daily meditation part of your everyday life. Fix a definite routine and stick to it at all costs. There should be perfect regularity in the hours of your spiritual practice. Affirm that you will meditate on a regular basis with a clear sense of purpose for living, and for realising your true Divine nature, for becoming established in the awareness of your innermost Self.

Meditate with specific intention; a firm resolve to accomplish the purpose of practice rather than be passive and not alertly focused.

When you decide to follow the spiritual path and follow a daily routine of meditation, you will need to make good use of your time by planning your waking hours – how to carry out your daily duties, how to wisely make good use of your spare time, minimising your unconscious thinking and activities and being more consciously aware and alert.

Sitting for Meditation

For your daily sitting meditation, choose a quiet and comfortable place that is clean, and ventilated, where you will not be disturbed, and which you will use regularly, and *only* for meditation. This will help to create a meditative vibration and a spiritual atmosphere in the place where you will sit. If it is possible, try to sit facing east or north. This is because the polarity of the Earth's magnetic field subtly influences us with a positive effect.

Sit upright in a comfortable and steady posture, facing east. Sitting in a cross-legged Yoga posture (*sukhāsana, siddhāsana, ardha-padmāsana,* or *padmāsana*) is most ideal, as these postures were naturally designed to direct the energy upwards in the spine to the higher centres of consciousness (*chakras*). But if you are unable to sit in these Yoga postures then sit upright on a straight-backed, armless chair without crossing your legs and without your back leaning against the back of the chair.

Begin the habit of sitting for meditation at the same time, in the same place, and for the full length of time that you have set for yourself every day. Once you have developed this habit, it will become easier to meditate. Then when you start to feel and experience the benefits of meditation – calmness, stillness, inner peace, inner joy, contentment and feeling the energy in your spine and brain – you will realise that meditation is actually your natural state of Being.

When to Meditate

You can meditate at any time when it is convenient, but the most powerful times to meditate are at sunrise, midday, sunset and midnight. It is at these times that the gravitational pull of the sun works in harmony with the natural polarity of the human body. Also, at these points of time nature becomes peaceful and there is a change in the flow of spiritual vibrations inside and outside us.

In India, the yogis say that the most auspicious and peaceful time to meditate in the morning is between 4 a.m. and 6 a.m. This auspicious time is known as *Brāhmamuhurta.*

If you want to meditate early in the morning, then make sure you go to bed early at around 10 p.m. Also eat lightly at night, so that your sleep is not disturbed by heavy digestion.

Length of Meditation

For the beginner, the duration of spiritual practice should be slowly and steadily increased. If you are new to meditation, then sit for only 15 minutes in the beginning. It is more important to develop the constant habit of meditating regularly with alert attention than to sit for an hour feeling bored and restless, or to sit for half an hour one day and not meditate for the next few days. Be consistent and regular in your practice. Begin with a daily 15-minute period of sitting for meditation and try to sit for this period once in the morning and once in the evening, so that you have two meditations a day. If you can do this without creating any mental tension or restlessness, and can remain calmly centred without moving your body, then increase the length of your meditation to 20 minutes, and practise once or twice a day. As you progress and find it more comfortable and relaxed to sit, then you can gradually increase the length of time you sit for your meditation. Ideally, to have a *deep* meditative experience, you will need to sit for 45 minutes or for one hour. The longer the better, but remember, it is the *quality* of your meditation that counts. The quality that gives you a deep sense of *inner calmness* and *stillness*, whilst feeling a *lightness of being,* an *ineffable peace* and *bliss.* This *direct* experience in deep meditation brings you to the realisation that you are not the mind, body or senses that undergo incessant change, but the changeless indwelling Self that transcends them. The Self is eternal and real by nature, whereas the body is transient and unreal.

Keeping Silence After Your Meditation

After your meditation, remain inwardly quiet and centred in the calm centre of your Self. Carry the inner peace, calmness and joy that you experience and feel from your meditation into your daily life, so that you experience your daily duties with awareness from the calmness of the inner Self. This will create a strong centre of calm and stillness within you as you go about your daily duties and relate to others, and it will give you great strength during challenging times.

Hong-Sau Technique of Concentration

"The Hong-Sau technique is a scientific method for
resting the heart, thereby increasing longevity,
and liberating a vast amount of Life Current, or
energy, to be distributed over the whole body,
renewing all the body cells and preventing their decay."
Paramhansa Yogananda.
(*The Wisdom of Yogananda*, Volume 7 –
'How to Awaken Your True Potential' (2015), Crystal Clarity Publishers,
Nevada City, California.)

An excellent technique for withdrawing your mind from the senses and internalising the attention, deepening the concentration and calming the mind in preparation for deep meditation is a technique in which you focus on the inhalation and exhalation with the two seed-syllable (*bīja*) mantra, *Hong-Sau* (pronounced as 'Hong-saw'). This *mantra* works on a pure vibrational level by stilling the mental energy in the form of restless thoughts and purifying the ego. *Hong-Sau* is the inner sound of the inhaling and exhaling breath. It also calms and interiorises the *prāṇa* in the body.

The mind can never be focused without a mental object. Therefore, you must give your mind an object that is readily available in every present moment. Your breath is the closest object. Every moment the breath is flowing in and flowing out through your nostrils. The concentration technique of *Hong-Sau* is practised by deeply concentrating intently on the breath with total attention trains the mind to stay focused like a 'one-pointed' laser beam. By training your mind to maintain a concentrated focus on a single point on the breath, whilst following it with the *mantra*, the other techniques and meditations that you practise will become increasingly deeper.

Hong-Sau means 'I am He', "I, the manifested Self, am He, the Unmanifested Spirit (the Absolute)." By consciously repeating mentally the seed-syllable mantra *Hong-Sau*, in conjunction with the concentration on the breath we affirm that the ego-self is one with the Infinite Spirit. *Hong* as the inhaling breath, represents the contraction of consciousness into finitude. *Sau* as the exhaling breath, represents the expansion of consciousness and the reabsorption of differentiation and separation into pure unity. In essence, *Hong-Sau* is the eternal, universal unspoken Primordial Vibration or Name of God. The Holy Name (Primordial Vibration) and God are One and all-permeating.

Hong-Sau is the natural sound of the breath – *Hong* with the inhalation, *Sau* with the exhalation. Throughout the 24 hours of the day, the breath flows in and out 21,600 times in a continuous mantra of *Hong-Sau*. Unknowingly, we are all repeating this mantra in a process of automatic and continuous recitation. In Yoga, continuous recitation of a mantra is called *ajapā-japa*. The *japa* becomes *ajapā*, when the mantra gets repeated in the mind on its own. The difference between *ajapā-japa* and *japa* is that *ajapā-japa* goes on subconsciously all the time, whilst *japa* is done consciously.

The great *Kriyā Yogi*, Paramhansa Yogananda (1893–1952) as a young boy named Mukunda, would sit in meditation and practise *Hong-Sau* meditation technique for seven hours at a time, until he achieved a deep breathless state. Yogananda said that we can reach states of spiritual bliss in longer, deeper practice of the *Hong-Sau* Technique, and that to become a master in this life, you should practice *Hong-Sau* for two hours a day. To master your mind and transform your life so that you become inwardly free, practise *Hong-Sau*.

Yogananda called *Hong-Sau*, 'the Baby *Kriyā*'. The actual *Kriyā* meditation technique that has been passed down through a succession of enlightened *Kriyā* Masters from Mahavatar Babaji to Paramhansa Yogananda, the Kuṇḍalinī life force flows in the spine and rises up through the *chakras* to the pituitary gland at the *ājñā* (the sixth chakra), and then it is offered to the Divine at the crown centre (*sahasrāra*) above the head.

"The purpose of the Hong-Sau technique is to help you to free your attention from outwardness, and to withdraw it from the senses, for breath is the cord that keeps the soul tied to the body... By dispassionately watching the breath coming in and going out, one's breathing naturally slows, calming at last the peace-disturbing activity of the heart, lungs, and diaphragm."

Paramhansa Yogananda.

(The Wisdom of Yogananda, Volume 7 – 'How to Awaken Your True Potential' (2015), Crystal Clarity Publishers, Nevada City, California.)

To prepare for this practice of *Hong-Sau*, follow this procedure:

Tensing and Relaxing

Sit in a comfortable and steady meditation posture with the head neck, and spine aligned. Relax the mind and body by inhaling deeply and holding the breath. Then whilst retaining your breath, tense all the muscles in your body. Hold both the breath and the tension in the muscles for a few seconds, then simultaneously release the breath and the tension, and relax. Repeat the process of tensing and relaxing three times, then finish by completely relaxing, and *feel* the relaxation and the flow of energy into the body.

Measured Breathing

Now continue to remain relaxed with your eyes closed, inwardly focused at the spiritual eye (midpoint between the eyebrows). Practise a minimum of six rounds of measured breathing. This is a three-part equal breath ratio of 6:6:6. Begin by inhaling through both nostrils to a slow count of six. Hold the breath in to a slow count of six, then exhale through your mouth to a slow count of six.

Sit Calmly for Meditation

Remain sitting still and concentrate your relaxed attention at the point between the eyebrows (spiritual eye). Let go of all thoughts and be totally centred in the present here and now moment. Place your hands palms upward on the knees in *Chin mudrā* (gesture of consciousness). Close your eyes and relax, with your awareness on the natural breath. Keep the body still and bring your attention and awareness to the frontal part of the brain at the point between the eyebrows (the Spiritual Eye, the seat of spiritual consciousness). If your mind wanders, gently bring it back to the practice of watching the breath with awareness. Watching the breath is a present-moment experience. Interiorise your mind by deepening your attentive awareness and concentration.

Hong-Sau – Technique of Concentration

The following practice of the *Hong-Sau* technique should be practised calmly, with relaxation, and with an attitude of reverence, for the mantra is one with God. There is no difference between God and his Name. The practice of *Hong-Sau* purifies your mind and connects you with God or the Self within.

Now with your body and mind still, uniting your mind with the present moment, begin the practice *Hong-Sau*. With closed eyes and without straining, gently lift your gaze upward to the point between the eyebrows, and with steady concentration and calmness look into the Spiritual Eye. Feel the natural breath flow in and out of the nostrils. Feel the tactile sensation of the breath and try to feel where the flow of breath is strongest in the nostrils. The sensation of breath is subtle, and yet it is quite distinct when you learn to tune into it. Once you have found the point where the breath is the strongest in the nostrils, (this is usually just inside the tip of the nose) then concentrate on the breath at that point. It is from this point that you will follow the whole passage of breath. Use this single point sensation inside the nose to keep your attention fixed. Observe each breath with attention and precision in present-moment awareness, taking it one split second on top of another. In this way, continuous and unbroken awareness will eventually result.

Then as your mind becomes calmer, begin to feel the sensation of the air that passes in and out of your nostrils higher up in the nasal passages by the point between the eyebrows, at the seat of *will* and concentration. As your concentration deepens your breathing will slow down, and you will be able to focus on it more clearly, with fewer and fewer interruptions. As you concentrate on your breath, make no attempt to control the breath. This is not a yoga breathing exercise. With the calm attitude of a *silent observer*, just let go and allow the natural process and flow of breathing go along at its own rhythm.

Inhale deeply, then slowly exhale. As the next inhalation naturally arises and flows into the nostrils, feel the breath where it enters the nostrils, and at the same time, mentally repeat the *bīja* (seed-syllable) *mantra* **Hong** (rhymes with 'song'). Imagine that the breath itself is making this sound. And as the breath flows out naturally of its own accord, at the same time mentally repeat the *mantra* **Sau** (rhymes with 'saw'). Make no attempt to control the breath, just allow its flow to be completely natural. Remember, the process of *Hong-Sau* is not a breathing technique or mental recitation exercise, it is simply being consciously aware with the concentration on the *Hong-Sau* mantra as the breath flows. The sound of the breath coming in and going out is the repetition of the *Hong-Sau* mantra. Feel that the breath itself is silently making the sounds of *Hong-Sau*. Continue gazing into the Spiritual Eye, the seat of spiritual consciousness, and as the breath naturally flows in simultaneously mentally repeat the *mantra* **Hong**. As the breath flows out, simultaneously mentally repeat the *mantra* **Sau**. By concentration on the breath, the breath gradually diminishes. This gradual subtle refinement leads naturally to an interiorised meditative state. When the mind is united with the breath flowing all the time, you will be able to focus the mind on the present moment.

If your attention wanders, or thoughts or feelings interfere with your concentration, be more alertly intentional and focused by keep bringing your attentive awareness and concentration back to the practice of Hong-Sau.

As you practise *Hong-Sau*, the vibration of the *inner Self*, you may become aware that the pauses or spaces between each breath are increasing. Follow your awareness: Now the breath is flowing in… Now the breath is still… Now the breath is flowing out… Now the breath is still… Now the breath is flowing in again… Now the breath is still… Be aware of this stillness – a fraction of a moment – between each breath and focus subtly on that fraction of a moment where both the breath and the syllables of the mantra arise and subside. The stillness of the breath occurs at the point where the breath is retained, which occurs naturally at the point where the breath is held. As these pauses or intervals of breath suspension between the breaths grow longer, enjoy the meditative bliss and expansion into the freedom of infinite spaciousness whilst inwardly gazing into your spiritual eye. By silently observing the breathless state, you let go of the identification with your body, and realise that you are something other than the mind-body-senses. You realise that your body is sustained by something other than the breath. In the timeless moment, the stillness in between breaths of the breathless state, you perceive the present moment of the Reality within you. This is the space of the *innermost Self*. Enjoy that experience of expansion into the freedom of infinite spaciousness whilst inwardly gazing into your spiritual eye. Then, when the breath naturally returns, continue with the practice of *Hong-Sau*.

During and after practising *Hong-Sau*, remain in the inner calmness for as long as possible. Remember and *feel* that inner calmness from your meditation, and remain calmly centred within your Self, allowing the calmness to permeate your everyday consciousness as you go about your daily activities. In this way, your mind will be filled with fresh spiritual thoughts and inspiration, and you will feel a higher joy. You will then be at peace with yourself and with the world around you.

Constantly remember that you are an immortal, spiritual being destined to be fully enlightened and liberated from all of the psychological conditions and influences that cloud your awareness and perception of your true nature and higher Reality. Aspire to be fully conscious and Self-aware, rather than want experiences that provide emotional comfort.

Hong-Sau Breathing in the Spine

For gaining awareness of the inner currents of energy in the spine

Once you have learned to practise *Hong-Sau* of focusing awareness on your breath at the nostrils and the Spiritual Eye, you can practise *Hong-Sau* in the spine. This will give you a greater awareness of the currents of energy flowing in your spine. Whereas *Hong-Sau* practised at the Spiritual Eye will deepen your concentration and give you inner calmness.

1. Sit in a comfortable and steady meditation posture with the head, neck, and spine aligned. Relax the mind and body by taking a few deep breaths. Place your hands palms upward on the knees in *Chin mudrā* ('gesture of consciousness' – of both hands the tip of the index finger touches the tip of the thumb, the other fingers are relaxed). Close your eyes and relax, with your awareness on the natural breath.

2. First, begin by practising *Hong-Sau* as you were taught before (see page 127) for about five minutes. Then, transfer your focused attention from watching the breath at the Spiritual Eye to concentrating and feeling the energy in your astral spine. You can imagine the astral spine to be like a hollow tube running through the centre of your body.

3. Concentrate on feeling the flow of energy in your spine. As it ascends from the base of the spine to the Spiritual Eye with the inhalation, mentally chant *Hong*. As the flow of energy in the spine descends with the exhalation, mentally chant *Sau*. Remember, you are not controlling your breath but only observing it with attentive awareness. When your practice deepens, you may find that the spaces between your breaths widen. You will be breathing less. If this happens, leave the technique and enjoy the calmness in these still moments. You can continue the practice when the breath begins again.

When your mind is calm and attention is focused, disregard forms of practice and techniques and rest in the deep silence and inner stillness of the Self. Remain with your inner gaze at the midpoint between the eyebrows at the spiritual eye. Being aware in the front and higher regions of the brain can help you to be focused and to transcend subconscious influences, memories and mental processes.

The techniques of meditation will help you to remove the obstacles of the mind so that you can go beyond the mind and thought to abide in Self-awareness. In that state of Self-awareness, concentrate on the inner joy or bliss (*ānanda*) that you feel and experience, because that is the essential nature of your spiritual Self. As you concentrate on that inner joy, it will begin to expand, and you will come to realise that it is your real spiritual nature – the Self.

Without any expectations of results, allow your spiritual awakening to occur naturally. *Direct experience* (without need of intellect, intuition, mind or the senses) with accurate Self-knowledge is liberating realisation – the culmination of deep meditation, spiritual aspiration, dedication to that aim, right living, effective spiritual practise and grace.

The Breathless State

By silently observing the breathless state, you let go of the identification with your body, and realise that you are something other than mind-body-senses. You realise that your body is sustained by something other than the gross breath. In the perfect stillness in between the breaths of the breathless state, you perceive the reality of pure consciousness within you.

This breathless state in which there are long pauses between the breaths, happens naturally. There is no need to be anxious or alarmed, for the breath returns automatically when the body needs to breathe again. Just remain calm and aware in the meditative stillness and inner freedom from body-consciousness, and allow the breath to effortlessly flow, stop and start naturally without any control by you.

Practising Hong-Sau in Daily Life

"Hold to the great calmness you feel during and after practice.
Cling to that peace as long as possible. Apply it in practical
life situations, when dealing with people, when studying,
when doing business, when thinking. And use it to help
practise self-control, when trying to rid yourself of
some deep-seated, harmful mental or emotional habits."
Paramhansa Yogananda.
(The Wisdom of Yogananda, Volume 7 –
'How to Awaken Your True Potential' (2015), Crystal Clarity Publishers,
Nevada City, California.)

Apart from sitting meditation, *Hong-Sau* can be used effectively in daily living situations. Here are some different ways of using the *Hong-Sau* technique:

• At times other than meditation time

Practise *Hong-Sau* during free or spare or at times other than meditation time – when you are not having to study, work or do anything that requires your concentration such as travelling on public transport (train, bus, aircraft or as a passenger in a car), and when you are sitting, waiting for your appointment (doctor, dentist) or an interview. As you sit resting, you can either keep your eyes closed (focused at the midpoint between the eyebrows) or open (focus your gaze on one point). Observe your breath mentally chanting *Hong* with the inhalation and *Sau* with the exhalation. This practice will help you to keep your mind calm and focused and free from mental restlessness.

• When you are nervous, restless or agitated

Sometimes you may find yourself in a nervous, restless or agitated state. To calm the mind of these states, sit quietly if possible and observe your breath, mentally repeat *Hong* as you inhale and *Sau* as you exhale. Even if you are outside walking, you can still calm your mind by observing your breath and mentally repeating *Hong-Sau*.

• When you are experiencing pain or suffering

If you are experiencing pain or suffering (physical, mental or emotional), observe your breath and mentally repeat *Hong* as you inhale and *Sau* as you exhale at the centre of the pain. This will help you not to identify yourself with the pain. It will help to reduce and may even dissolve the pain.

• To resolve or solve a problem and to raise your consciousness

Hong-Sau can also be practised to resolve or solve a problem, and to raise your consciousness. As you observe your breath, focus your attention at the medulla oblongata at the back of the brain (the centre of ego-consciousness), and as you inhale mentally repeat *Hong* and feel the energy gathering at the medulla. As you exhale, mentally repeat *Sau*, and offer the energy up to your spiritual eye (at the midpoint between the eyebrows).

Listening to the Cosmic Vibration *Aum*

"Patanjali speaks of God (in the Yoga Sutras 1:27) as the actual Cosmic Sound of Aum heard in meditation. Aum is the Creative Word, the sound of the Vibratory Motor. Even the yogi-beginner soon inwardly hears the wondrous sound of AUM. Receiving this blissful spiritual encouragement, the devotee becomes assured that he is in actual touch with divine realms."
Paramhansa Yogananda.
Autobiography of a Yogi, Original 1946 Edition.

Aum (pronounced as *Oṁ when chanted*), also known as the *Praṇava*, is the Divine Cosmic Vibration that *is* God. In the Bible, the *Word* that St John refers to is the Creative Vibration: *"In the beginning was the Word, and the Word was with God and the Word was God.*" (John 1:1). And similarly, in the *Vedas,* it is said: "*In the beginning Prajapati, or the Lord of Creation, alone existed; He alone was the universe; He had Vak as His own and as second to Him, and Vak, or the Word, was verily the Supreme Brahman.*"

There are numerous names, words and symbols used to symbolise God. But there is no other word that can convey the significance and *direct* experience of the Ultimate Reality so profoundly and accurately as the word-sound symbol, *Aum (Oṁ)*. Even the word God in comparison to *Aum* is insufficient and limited in its function and significance.

After practising the *Hong-Sau* technique, and afterwards sitting still in meditation, feeling the inner calmness for some time, you will be ready to listen to, and become absorbed in the Cosmic Vibration, *Aum (Oṁ)*.

The *Aum* Technique

In this meditation technique, the energy that normally flows out through the senses is redirected within. The outer senses of seeing and hearing are closed by using a hand *mudrā*, so that the awareness and attention can be attuned inwardly to perceive the subtle sounds of *Aum (Oṁ)*. When your mind is interiorised with your awareness focused midpoint between the eyebrows at the spiritual eye, and concentrated there for some time, it awakens the subtle sounds of the *chakras*. The mind then becomes deeply absorbed in these inner subtle astral sounds, leading to the pure sound of *Aum*. At first you may only hear the sounds of your own physical body, like your heart beating; blood pumping through your veins; or the sound of you breathing, but as your consciousness is withdrawn deeper within you may hear the astral sounds emanating from your *chakras* in the astral spine, which can draw you still deeper into the all-compelling, all-captivating and all-absorbing cosmic sound of *Aum*. Deeply merged in the vibrationless calm of *Aum* one can enter into the blissful and expansive state of *samādhi* in oneness with the Ultimate Reality; God.

Your inner attunement to the Cosmic Sound of *Aum* can also attract the grace and presence of divine light. Also manifested in the Divine are the qualities of: divine love, heavenly bliss, ineffable peace, perfect wisdom, perfect calmness and stillness.

This meditation of inner perception – listening with the ear of intuition – to the Cosmic Vibration of *Aum* is best practised when the mind is calm and focused in the stillness after practising *Hong-Sau* meditation. For beginners, practise *Hong-Sau* for at least three months to help you deepen your concentration and calm the restlessness of the mind, before you start to practise this *Aum* Inner Sound Meditation. Then you will be able to go deep in your meditation to feel a deep sense of inner calmness, and attunement in oneness with Ultimate Reality; God.

1. First, allow your body to become calm and steady and your thoughts to settle down. Allow your heart to become attentive to the sound of the natural breath. Then, calm the mind and deepen your concentration by practising the *Hong-Sau* technique for 10 to 15 minutes, or until you are calmly centred within in inner stillness.

2. Sit in a comfortable meditation posture with your head, neck and spine aligned. Place your upper arms on a wooden 'T-shaped' armrest, parallel to the floor with your elbows in line with your shoulders. Make sure the arms and shoulders are at a comfortable height. There should be no strain on your hands, arms, back or neck. Another alternative is to use earplugs to close the ears, which are available from pharmacist shop.

3. Raise your hands up to your head and position the fingers in the *Aum mudrā*: first close your ears by gently pressing the earflaps (*tragi*) inward with your thumbs. Rest the little fingers gently and lightly on the outer corners of each closed eyelid. Rest the other fingers on the forehead pointing inward toward the point between the eyebrows to direct energy toward the Spiritual Eye.

4. Whilst holding the *Aum mudrā* breathe normally, and with your eyes closed, gaze with deep attentive awareness into the Spiritual Eye. Then in a natural rhythm, mentally chant *Aum, Aum, Aum, Aum*...continuously at the Spiritual Eye, so that it vibrates and resonates in that centre.

5. As you gaze inwardly, into the Spiritual Eye mentally chanting *Aum*, simultaneously listen in your right ear for the subtle inner sound-frequencies of the *chakras* in the astral spine. If you hear the sounds in the left ear, gradually bring them to your right ear. If you hear one

distinct sound, focus your awareness totally on that one sound. As sensitivity develops, another fainter sound will be heard behind it. Leave the first sound and transfer your awareness to the fainter sound. Again, a third sound will be begin to emerge behind the second sound. With awareness, continue discarding the grosser sounds for the more subtle sounds. Your aim is to reach the source of all sound – the Primordial Sound, *Aum.* As your listening to *Aum* deepens, your consciousness expands, and you begin to feel omnipresent, beyond the mind, body, ego and the senses. Your consciousness dissolves into that omnipresent *Aum* sound-current of the power of Consciousness, and you feel complete oneness with *Aum*, experiencing the reality of Supreme Consciousness, God.

6. After listening to the inner sound vibration of *Aum*, remain sitting calmly and joyfully in the stillness of your meditation, beyond time and space, and experience pure awareness of *Being* or a perception of oneness with the Divine, that source of bliss that lies *within* you. Know and realise that you are timeless, spaceless, beyond the mind-body-senses.

Stay connected to the Infinite by continuing to hold in mind the peaceful after-effects of your meditation as you go about your day. Mentally affirm to yourself, "*I am Consciousness, I am Bliss, I am the eternal changeless Self.*"

The Inner Sounds of the Chakras

"In the beginning stage of the practice, one hears different types of strong or gross inner sounds. When the practice increases one hears subtle and subtler sounds."
Nādabindūpaniṣad, 33

As a beginner, when you first practise the *Aum* Inner Sound Meditation you may only hear the inner sounds of the physical body: heartbeat, blood circulation and breathing. You may also hear a very high-pitched electrical sound from the electrical field of energy of the astral body. If you hear any of these distinct sounds, then concentrate on them until they recede into the background, then transfer your awareness to the next fainter sound that you hear, and then to the more subtle astral sounds. If your mind is deeply interiorised and calm whilst listening to these inner sounds, you will eventually be able to tune into and hear the subtle sounds of the *chakras* in the astral spine. Listening to the inner *chakra* sounds will lead you to hear the Primordial Sound vibration, *Aum*.

In the *Hamsopaniṣad, 16,* the classical ten different inner sounds are described: sounds of the honeybee or bumblebee, crickets singing in the forest, sound of a temple bell, blowing of a conch shell, sound of stringed instruments

135

(like a lute, harp, vina, sitar or tamboura), cymbals, flute, double ended drum like a *mridaṅga*, a low-pitched drum and the roar of thunder.

The Chakra Sounds as Heard in Meditation

Mūladhāra chakra – The humming or drone of bees, a low vibratory sound. When heard less perfectly it may sound like a motor or a drum.

Svādhiṣṭhāna chakra – Like a Flute. When heard less perfectly it may sound like Crickets singing in the forest, or like running water of a mountain spring.

Maṇipūra chakra – Stringed instrument sound, like a sitar or harp.

Anāhata chakra – Like the flowing peal of deep bells, or a gong. Less perfectly, it sounds like tinkling bells.

Viśuddha chakra – Thunder or the ocean's roar. When heard less perfectly it may sound of wind or a waterfall.

Ājñā chakra (spiritual eye/medulla) – A symphony of sounds; *Aum*.

> *"Brahman is beyond the silence, the state is of the*
> *Supreme Self (Paramātmā). Whilst there is sound there*
> *is the mind, at the end of sounds the mind does not exist."*
> **Nādabindūpaniṣad, 48**

When the mind concentrates on the subtle inner sounds, it recognises the different types of sounds, but still the mind has not been transcended. It is only when the mind completely merges with the subtle sounds that both the subtle sounds and the mind cease to exist. The ultimate goal is for the Self (*Atman*) to merge in the *Brahman* (God) the universal Consciousness, 'That' which is beyond all sounds, and which is to be known and realised.

All that we experience and perceive in this world is dependent upon there being both a subject and an object, or a seer and a seen. Nothing can be experienced or perceived without the subject, the seer. And vice-versa, if there is only an object without a subject or seer to perceive it nothing is experienced. If a tree falls in the stillness of a forest, and no one hears it fall, was there really a sound?

Spiritual Progress

After engaging in spiritual practice and meditation for a short period of time, often the question arises, 'Have I made spiritual progress?' or 'How much progress have I made since I started meditation?'

First, we need to understand that the inner Self, our true identity, our essential Being, is pure, ever perfect and ever the same. It does not need improving, for the Self is complete, whole and perfect as it is. It cannot progress or regress, and nothing needs to be added to it or taken from it. The Self cannot be known by the intellect because the intellect is itself empowered by the Self. You perceive the activity of the mind by the light of the Self. You are the eternal Self - that consciousness with which you experience your very own existence - it is not something you have to attain.

So, what is actually meant by the term 'spiritual progress'? What needs improving, removing, or changing? And how can we measure our progress?

Let us think of measuring our progress in terms of improving the quality not of our inner Self, but of our mind. For a mind that is conditioned, restless, scattered, non-attentive and ruled by bad habits and attachment to desires can never gather enough momentum to make spiritual progress.

You can measure your own spiritual progress by improving the quality of your mind. You will need to make a great and determined effort with *willpower* and *energy* and patience to succeed. One-pointedness of mind through concentration and meditation is an important requisite to help you accomplish that. Without gathering together and concentrating the energy of the mind, the deeper state of meditation is not possible.

It takes *willingness* and *willpower*, and a *strong, persistent effort*, to overcome the habits that keep us enslaved to our desires, negative attitudes, negative thinking and wrong behaviour.

Make the effort now! Be very vigilant! Do not allow your sensory desires, habits and environment to control you. Discipline your body, your mind and its thoughts and words, so that the qualities and virtues of your inner Self can be revealed.

Many people do not change or progress in their life because they do not see their own faults. They are ruled by their habits, impulses, desires, attachments, and self-limiting idiosyncrasies, which keep them in bondage, in ignorance of their true spiritual nature.

To change, progress, and be successful, it is important to *introspect*, to look at yourself and your life. Look at your habits, desires and attachments. Ask yourself what is standing in your way and holding you back. What are the shortcomings in your character and your life that are impeding you? Make an introspective list by dispassionately writing down your thoughts and aspirations, so that you can see the thought-patterns, habits and desires that are holding you in bondage. Then, using your discriminative wisdom you will be able to discern what is happening and break the negative patterns that make you behave in a certain way.

Be willing to renounce mental attitudes, feelings, behaviours, habits, and circumstances that confine your awareness and limit your ability to freely, creatively function. Transcend and avoid being unduly influenced by inertia that dulls the intellect and mind. This can be done by intentionally performing useful actions rather than be impelled by restlessness, emotions, or whims; constant aspiration to be fully, spiritually awake; nurturing your total wellbeing; and frequent, deep meditation practice.

Affirmation: *By turning within in meditation and prayer for divine guidance, I have the assurance that I am following the path that is right for me.*

I live with higher purpose in accord with my higher aspiration to do what supports my goal to live mindfully with awareness of my essential nature and my relationship with the Divine and all of life. All of my thoughts and actions confirm my commitment to my spiritual path. As an immortal spiritual being, I live in freedom, in joy, peace, and love. I am healthy, happy, and creatively expressive.

Indications of Spiritual Progress in Meditation and one's life

1. During meditation you experience a deep inner calmness. The mind becomes still with ineffable peace and inner joy or bliss.

2. Increased enthusiasm and love for meditation. The more you meditate the more you want to meditate. Your daily meditation becomes your most important engagement and an indispensable part of each day.

3. There is an absence of restlessness and agitation. The mind is attentive, has clarity, and is consciously aware. There is definite, undivided effort and attention.

4. A sense of oneness rather than separation from our divine Source. It is understanding that you are transcending duality, transcending the misunderstanding, that you are separate from your own divine Source - the Blissful Self within you.

5. Spiritual progress is authenticated by your character and behaviour as you begin to perceive and develop noble and divine qualities - truthfulness, love, inner peace and care for all beings.

6. Increased one-pointed awareness and unwavering commitment to living in Truth. There is a sense of dedication, self-offering, and devotion towards the spiritual ideal you are following.

7. An expansion of consciousness, experiencing a oneness of unconditional love, peace, contentment, and harmony towards all beings and all life.

8. Every moment of life is utilised for meditation. The inner subjective state becomes important, not the outer circumstances. One has a strong conviction to act on a calm intuitive state of inner perception.

9. The mind becomes calm and steady as you have control over your thoughts, emotions, speech and actions. A meditator knows success when he transforms his character and reduces his desires, bad habits and sense-attachments to bring balance and harmony to his daily life.

10. The mind turns from a limited, contractive ego-self - criticising and judging others, negative thinking, selfishness, unkindness, carelessness - to a more expansive consciousness that is positive, giving one a more compassionate and empathetic outlook towards others, an awareness of changelessness amidst change, and a deeper self-understanding.

11. As the obstacles of the mind - karmas, habits, desires, thoughts, emotions, attitudes, influences and associations - to higher consciousness and awareness are removed, one is then able to live their life in a higher consciousness.

12. When the mind and heart are purified through Kriya Yoga Meditation, and the mind is steady, and is able to discriminate wisely allowing remembrance of the Self, then there is freedom from bondage (ignorance).

Epilogue
Aspire to a Higher Goal in Life

"The Kingdom of God is within you."
– The Bible, Luke 17:21.

"Be still and know that 'I am' God"
– The Bible, Psalms 46:10.

*"Seek first the kingdom of God (within you) and every other thing will be
added unto you."*
– The Bible, Luke 12:31.

Once you have a higher aspiration, a higher goal in life to awaken spiritually, and have made a sincere commitment to practising Yoga and meditation to realise your own true nature, remain steadfast in your resolve. Be determined to succeed, to become established in the highest Truth. Practise this without faltering, until it becomes a reality and you find true happiness and freedom. Do not waste your mental and spiritual powers on superficial or non-useful interests.

The spiritual path of Yoga and meditation is not for the weak-minded or the faint-hearted, it requires a determined, strong, persistent and sustained effort over a long period of time, to remove the turbulence of the mind – restlessness, desires, likes and dislikes, bad habits, wrong attitudes, attachments and sense-indulgence. This requires self-discipline and daily spiritual practice (*sādhana*) – you practice *sādhana* to discover the truth of your own nature, to know your inner Self. The natural and constant state of the Self is joy, peace and happiness. By meditating and attentively focusing on your own inner joy, you open the gate to the inner Kingdom of God.

Paramhansa Yogananda said: *"Most people are half-hearted in their thoughts and actions – hence, they do not succeed. A mental habit, in order to materialise, must be strong and persistent."*

Nourish your Yoga and meditation practice with fresh inspiration and *enthusiasm* on a daily basis, and nurture that experience in every way you can. Accomplish purposes that are of value to your well-being and the well-being of others and the environment.

Remain steadfast on the spiritual path, aspire to *know* and *realise* the Truth, that you may experience the Supreme Reality, the divinity that dwells *within* you. Live wisely as a conscious, spiritually aware person in harmony and peace with all life. To see inner peace, you must constantly work on your perception of the world and other people, by seeing the Divine in all, seeing unity in diversity, and seeing oneness instead of duality, for it is duality and ignorance that is the cause of all suffering. As long as there is duality and division, there can be no peace or harmony.

Remember your infinite omnipresent nature

"Self-Realisation is the knowing in all parts of body, mind,
and soul that you are now in possession of the kingdom of God;
that you do not have to pray that it come to you; that God's
omnipresence is your omnipresence; and that all you
need to do is improve your knowing."
Paramhansa Yogananda.

Constantly remind yourself and sustain the awareness that you are not the limiting mind-body-senses or ego-personality. Affirm: "*I am Consciousness, I am Bliss, I am the changeless, ever-present Self.*" Always remain aware of and identify with your true nature, the blissful, changeless Self within you, that is eternally free, the witness of the thoughts and feelings that move through the mind, and yet is not affected by them. Acknowledging your true nature and your relationship with the Infinite will help bring forth your divine qualities. Remember, that throughout every instant of your life, through every experience, there has been one thing that has always been constant, one thing is unchanging, within all of your changes of life. That thing is your own silent *Awareness*, the witnessing Self. It is still and silent. It is eternal, changeless, timeless, formless, and without limitation. It is ever-existent, ever-conscious, ever-new bliss (*sat-cit-ānanda*). The very nature of the inner Self is love, peace and joy, and you are *That*.

True and lasting happiness will come to you only when you realise God *within*, when you experience the truth of your own Divine nature or being. Gain right understanding, wisdom and divine awareness. Cultivate peace of mind, emotional stability, calmness and cheerfulness, and live from that joy and freedom that you experience in deep meditation. Cultivate the habit of constant Self- and God-remembrance and support it with daily inspired and dedicated meditation. Live with a clear sense of higher purpose and do what is needed to enhance your total wellbeing and spiritual awareness. Live confidently and with certainty that God is always with you, and that God's energy is flowing in and through you, supporting your vitality. You are supported by that supreme and Divine Energy.

Be a true example of harmony, peace and love in the world

"Affirm divine calmness and peace, and send out
only thoughts of love and goodwill if you
want to live in peace and harmony."
Paramhansa Yogananda.

Nurture your mind with positive and constructive thoughts, and cultivate emotional calmness and stability, cheerfulness, faith and confidence, and radiate those positive qualities to others. Be inwardly peaceful regardless of what occurs so you can always be mentally calm and rational. Live in harmony and peace with others. Compassionately wish and pray for the highest good for everyone – for their complete wellbeing, harmonious circumstances, peace, happiness, abundance, prosperity and spiritual awakening.

Peace and Harmony Prayer

Paramhansa Yogananda has given us a wonderful prayer for affirming and visualising peace and harmony in ourselves and in the world, which can be practised anytime. An ideal time though is to practise the prayer for peace and harmony after the stillness of your meditation, when your mind is calm and peaceful.

Close your eyes and remain in the peaceful stillness of your meditation. Visualise the calm inner peace and harmony that you feel going out from you to the whole world. Repeat aloud ten times:

"Lord, fill this world with peace and harmony, peace and harmony."

Then, visualise peace inside yourself. Repeat aloud:

"Lord, fill me with peace and harmony."

Finally, raise your hands with your palms facing outwards and chant *Aum* aloud three times to send out peaceful and harmonies blessings to the world.

I close with Paramhansa Yogananda's beautiful and meaningful prayer that can be effective in restoring harmony and peace to us all. If you regularly meditate and sincerely pray on a daily basis – to become harmonious, peaceful, compassionate, loving and awaken to Self- and God-realisation, you will be living your life purpose in the highest way.

"May Thy love shine forever on the sanctuary of my devotion and may I be able to awaken that love in all hearts."

Aum shanti, shanti shanti.
Aum peace, peace, peace.

Guide to Sanskrit Pronunciation

Too often, in Western books on *Yoga*, there is an oversimplification of translation of a Sanskrit word into English, where the original meaning tends to get diluted, mistranslated, or lost. In this book, I have tried to keep as many Sanskrit words as possible in their original meaning.

Since the late 18th century, Sanskrit has been transliterated using the Latin alphabet. The system most commonly used today is the IAST (International Alphabet of Sanskrit transliteration), which has been the academic standard since 1888/1912.

The following guide to pronunciation gives approximate equivalents in English to the Sanskrit sounds.

Diacritical marks used in this translation

ā ī ū ṛ ḷ ḥ ṁ ṅ ñ ṇ ṭ ḍ ś ṣ

Vowels

a ā i ī u ū ṛ ṝ l ḹ e ai o au

These vowels are further divided into simple vowels (*a, ā,* and so on) and combined vowels (*e, ai, o, au*). The simple vowels are listed in pairs (*a-ā, i-ī...*). In each pair, the first vowel is short and the second is exactly twice as long. In the English transliteration the long vowels are marked with a bar (-). The diphthongs are also pronounced twice as long as the short vowels. Thus, in the words *nī - la* 'blue' or *go - pa* 'cowherd', the first syllable is held twice as long as the second.

Simple

a short *a* as in 'about'
ā long *a* as in 'father'
i short *i* as **e** in 'England'
ī long *i* as in **ee** in 'feet'
u short *u* as in **oo** in 'foot'
ū long *u* as in 'rule'
ṛ as in 'written' (but held twice as long)
ḷ **le** as in 'turtle'
ḹ longer '**le**'

Diphthongs

e as in 'they'
ai as in '**aisle**' '**ice**' 'kite'
o as in 'go'
au as in '**owl**'

Aspiration

ḥ (*visarga*) a final "h" sound that echoes the preceding vowel slightly; as in "aha" for *aḥ; iḥ* as ihi; *uḥ* as uhu.

Nasalised vowel

ṁ (*anusvara* - marked with a dot) a nasal sound pronounced like *mm*, but influenced according to whatever consonant follows, a in "bingo." The nasal is modified by the following consonant: *sāṁkhya* as saankhya.

Consonants

Consonants are generally pronounced as in English, but there are some differences. Sanskrit has many 'aspirated' consonants; these are pronounced with a slight *h* sound. For example, the consonant *ph* is pronounced as English *p* followed by an *h* as in ha*ph*azard. The *bh* is as in a*bh*or.

k as in 'skip'
kh as in '**Eckh**art'
g as in '**game**'
gh as in '**dogh**ouse'
ṅ as in 'si**ng**'
c as in 'ex**ch**ange'
ch as in '**church**'
j as in '**jam**'
jh a in 'he**dgeh**og'
ñ as in 'ca**ny**on'
ṭ as in '**t**ub', the tongue curls back and hits the upper palate
ṭh as in 'ligh**t-h**eart', the tongue curls back and hits the upper palate
ḍ **as in '**dove'**,** the tongue curls back and hits the palate
ḍh as in 'a**dh**ere', the tongue curls back and hits the palate
ṇ as in '**t**int', tip of tongue touches the back of the upper teeth
t as i '**t**ub', tip of tongue touches the back of the upper teeth
th as in '**th**ick', tip of tongue touches the back of the upper teeth
d as in '**d**ove' tip of tongue touches the back of the upper teeth
dh as in 're**d-h**ot', tip of tongue touches the back of the upper teeth
n as in '**n**ame', tip of tongue touches the back of the upper teeth
p as in '**p**apa'
ph as in 'ha**ph**azard'

144

b as in 'balloon'
bh as in 'abhor'
m as in 'mum'
y as in 'yellow'
r as in 'run'
l as in 'love'
v as in 'vine'
ś as in 'shell'
ṣ as in 'silk'
h as in 'hill'

Double consonants

In double consonants, both letters are pronounced distinctly separately.

śraddhā (faith) is pronounced *śrad-dhā*

icchā (desire) is pronounced *ic-chā*

jagannātha (Lord of the Universe) is pronounced *jagan-nātha*.

jña (to know) as in *jñana yoga* (the path of wisdom or higher knowledge) is widely pronounce 'gya'. More accurate is 'gnya', and best is to combine a correct *ja* with a correct *ña*.

Sanskrit Glossary

A

Abhāsya: Persistent repeated practice.

Agnisar kriya: Agni means 'fire' and *sara* means 'wash', so it literally means to wash the fire chakra (*Manipura Chakra*) located at the navel centre. This Yoga exercise also stimulates the immune system, increases the power of digestion and increases heat in the body, burning off toxins. It works by creating a 'vacuum' effect and strongly pulling and releasing the abdomen. This exercise is similar to *uddiyana bandha.*

Ājñā chakra: The sixth *chakra,* located at the eyebrow centre. It has two poles: the negative pole is at the medulla oblongata; the positive pole is at the midpoint between the eyebrows, the spiritual eye. The seat of concentration.

Anando'ham: mantra meaning 'I am Bliss.'

Anāhata chakra: Heart *chakra,* the fourth centre in the *suṣumnā,* the subtle spine.

Āsana: Seat, posture; pose for meditation, the third of eight limbs of *Aṣṭāṅga Yoga*).

Ashta-prakritis: earth, water, fire, air, ether, mind, intellect and ego.

Ātma; Ātman: The innermost Self, or soul.

Aum – The primordial mantra sound vibration of creation.

B

Bhāgavad Gītā: The word *Bhāgavad* refers to *Bhāgavan,* meaning 'God', and *Gītā* means 'song' – 'The Song of God' is an episode in the great epic *Mahābharata.* The fundamental philosophical viewpoints in the *Bhāgavad Gītā* are that: al existence is a manifestation of God; God exists in all beings as their inner Self; knowledge of and union with the Self is the supreme goal of life; and ignorance of our Divinity is the cause of our suffering.

Brāhmamuhurta: auspicious and peaceful time to meditate in the morning between 4 a.m. and 6 a.m.

Brāhman: From the Sanskrit verb root *brha,* meaning expansion, knowledge, all-pervasiveness. It indicates the Absolute Supreme Consciousness, that Absolute Reality.

Brahmacharya Vidyalaya: Brahmacharya literally means "going after Brahman (Supreme Reality, Self or God). *Vidyalaya* refers to the place where knowledge is spread or given such as a school, university or ashram.

C

Citta: mind-field; mind, field of consciousness.

D

Dharana: concentration

Dharma: 'that which holds together', 'righteousness', 'right action', 'duty'. There are two kinds of *dharma*: the duty to the Self, *svadharma*, which is the supreme duty, and our social or professional duties. Each person has his or her own *dharma* or duty to follow.

Dhyāna: meditation.

H

Hong-Sau – Kriya Yoga mantra, that calms the mind and deepens the concentration leading to meditation. *Hong-Sau* means "I am He", "I, the manifested Self, am He, the Unmanifested Spirit (the Absolute)."

Hṛdaya: The spiritual heart.

J

Jāgrat (waking state): conscious mind, beta waves.

K

Karma: Actions that have a binding effect; the law of cause and effect.

Kriya Yoga: the universal science of God-realisation. Kriyā Yoga: Kri from the sanskrit root Kriyā means 'to do, to act'. Kriyā Yoga is 'union with the Infinite through the action of Kriyā'. An ancient sacred Yoga science, that includes advanced techniques of meditation that leads to Self and God realisation. Kriyā Yoga was revived in this age by Mahavatar Babaji and passed down through a succession of Masters to Paramhansa Yogananda.

Kuṇḍalinī Śakti: Kundala means 'coiled'. *Śakti* means primordial cosmic energy. The coiled-up, dormant, primordial cosmic energy that gives power and energy to all the *chakras*, lies dormant at the *mūladhāra chakra*, at the base of the spine.

L

Lauliki nauli: abdominal rolling of the rectus muscle (*dakshina nauli* is isolating the right rectus muscle in the roll like movement from side to side, and *vama nauli* is to the left.

M

Manipura chakra: Maṇipūra means 'Jewelled City'. The third chakra located at the navel centre in the astral spine.

Mridaṅga: –a double ended Indian drum.

Mūladhāra chakra: The first chakra, at the base of the spine.

Mudrā: Mudrā means 'Gesture'. A *mudrā* is an energy seal that helps in controlling the *prāṇic* energy in the body.

N

Nāḍīs: Nāḍī means 'Flow'. Subtle nerve channels in the subtle body, through which the *prāṇic* energy flows.

P

Paramātmā: Supreme Self

Patañjali Yoga Sūtras: An authoritative text on Yoga. 196 aphorisms compiled prior to 400 CE by the Sage Patanjali that outline the eight limbs of Yoga. The Yoga Sutras give guidelines for living a meaningful and purposeful life with the ultimate aim of Self and God-realisation.

Prāṇa: vital life force; the universal all-permeating force of Nature which vibrates through all life and sustains the universe. Prāṇa is the vital link between the gross and the subtle world. Prāṇa is an intelligent force, but has no consciousness in the empirical, nor transcendental sense. It is the basis of the empirical consciousness, but soul is the conscious unit.

Praṇava: Praṇava means 'sounding' or 'reverberating' and refers to the vibration of consciousness itself. The Praṇava, the primordial sound vibration, a mantra that symbolises God. It is the supreme verbal symbol of Brahman both as the Absolute and as the personal God (Iśvara). It is written as Aum, and repeated or chanted as Oṁ.

Prāṇāyama: life control, expansion of vital energy.

Pratyahara: withdrawal of the senses.

R

Rajoguṇa: quality of activity or passion.

S

Sādhana: (from the root verb *sadh*, 'to accomplish one's goal, 'or 'to hit the target'). 'Spiritual practice' that is practised regularly for attainment of realisation of the Self, and cosmic consciousness.

Saṁskāras: Latent impressions stored in the subtle body and subconscious mind; deep mental impressions produced by past experiences; dormant impressions of our past lives; innate tendency.

Śavasana: corpse pose, relaxation pose lying down on the back.

Śanti: (pronounced 'shanti') means 'peace'.

Sivo'ham: mantra meaning 'I am Shiva', the all-pervasive, Supreme Reality.

Sat-Cit-Ānanda: existence, Consciousness, and Bliss absolute, or as Yogananda referred to it – *ever-Conscious, ever-Existent, ever-new Bliss.*

Samādhi: (*Sam* 'with'; *ādhi* 'Lord': 'union with the Lord'. Or *sam-ā-dhā* to hold together, to concentrate upon). The state of superconscious absorption that is attained when the meditator, the process of meditation and the object of meditation (God) become One.

Sattvic: One of the three qualities (*gunas*) of *Prakriti*, or nature, which are *rajas* (passion), *tamas* (dullness, inertia), and sativa (goodness or purity). *Sattvic* is an adjective that describes something or someone that has a pure, balanced and harmonious nature.

So'ham: mantra meaning 'I am That'.

Suṣumnā: The main subtle channel running through the spine, along which the six *chakras* are located. When awakened, the *Kuṇḍalinī Śakti* rises upward through the *Suṣumnā.*

Suṣupti (deep sleep state): unconscious mind, delta waves.

Svādhiṣṭhāna chakra: the second chakra located in the pelvic region of the astral spine.

Svapna (dream state): subconscious mind, alpha and theta waves.

Svayam-prakāsha: self-luminous.

T

Tadasana: Mountain pose, a standing yoga posture. In this pose you stand straight like a mountain, firm and strong at the base and ascending upwards. The standing *āsanas* all start from this position.

Tapasyā: *tapas* means 'heat' – the fire that burns up the impurities of the mind and body. *Tapasyā* means austerity.

Turīya: transcendental superconsciousness, the state beyond the three states of waking, dream and deep sleep.

U

Uḍḍīyana bandha: Abdominal Lock. A Hatha Yoga exercise that involves, after having exhaled all the air out, pulling the abdomen upward to create a vacuum in which the abdominal muscles and viscera move up to the thorax. The practice of *Uḍḍīyana bandha* strengthens the abdominal muscles and diaphragm, stimulates and lifts the energy of the lower belly (*apana vayu*), to unite it with the energies localised in the navel (*samana vayu*) and heart (*prana vayu*).

V

Vairāgya: Detachment; dispassion; freedom from worldly desires.

Vayu: 'vital air'. *Prāṇa* is known as *vayu,* or 'vital air', when it operates within the human body systems. The five main vital airs in the body – prāna, apāna, samāna, vyāna, and udāna.

Viśuddha chakra: The fifth chakra, which corresponds to the cervical plexus at the level of the throat.

Vṛttis: subtle vortices of energy created by samskāras, karmic actions, and waves of like and dislike that create our mental tendencies desires and habits, enter the subconscious mind and then get submerged in the lower chakras.

Y

Yamas and *Niyamas:* the moral precepts of Patañjali's 'Eight Limbs of Yoga'.

Yoga: The Sanskrit word Yoga comes from the Sanskrit root *yuj,* which means to yoke, join, unite, harness. Yoga signifies both the means and the end. It is the aim of human existence. The ultimate meaning is the union between the individual self and the universal Self. It is establishing oneness between the finite and the infinite, between the inner being and the Supreme Being.

Yogoda: The word '*Yogoda*' is derived from the Sanskrit word '*Yoga*' meaning union; and '*da*' meaning 'that which imparts'. *Yogoda* means a system of Yoga that imparts harmony, equilibrium and unity to the mind, body and soul. *Sat* means 'truth', and *Sanga* means 'community' or 'assembly'.

Yogaś citta vṛtti nirodhaḥ: From *Patañjali Yoga Sūtras,* sutra 1:2 means: 'Yoga (the experience of Unity) results from the neutralisation of ego-feelings (that produce the thought-waves in the mind).'

Bibliography

Autobiography of a Yogi – Paramhansa Yogananda.

The original 1946 unedited edition of Yogananda's spiritual masterpiece. Crystal Clarity Publishers, 14618 Tyler Foote Road, Nevada City, CA 95959. **www.crystalclarity.com**

Autobiography of a Yogi is a classic and one of the best-selling Yoga titles of all times, with millions of copies sold. This highly prized reprinting of the original 1946 edition is the only one available that is free from textual changes made after Yogananda's death. Yogananda was the first Kriya Yoga master to live and teach in the West.

The Yoga Book – Stephen Sturgess.

Watkins Publishing, London. **www.watkinspublishing.co.uk**

The Yoga Book is a core text – it explains the true meaning of Yoga and demonstrates the practices and postures of Patanjali's Ashtanga Yoga (The Eight Limbs of Yoga) that enable the reader to achieve mastery over the mind and body and can eventually lead to Self-Realisation. Through the practice of Yoga, we can directly bring stillness to the restless mind and body giving a true, lasting happiness from inner peace and contentment. The practices include: asana, pranayama, mudras, bandhas and meditation practices. Included in the foreword of his book *'What is Yoga?'*, Swami Kriyananda (a direct disciple of Paramhansa Yogananda) clearly explains the true meaning of Yoga.

The Book of Chakras & Subtle Bodies – Stephen Sturgess.

Watkins Publishing, London. **www.watkinspublishing.co.uk**

The Book of Chakras and Subtle Bodies offers detailed information and techniques for delving deeper into Yogic philosophy and well-being.
The book includes Raja and Kriya Yoga techniques, yoga asanas, mudras, bandpass, pranayama, mantras and meditation practices.

Yoga Meditation – Stephen Sturgess.

Watkins Publishing, London. **www.watkinspublishing.co.uk**

Practised authentically, all Yoga practices are preparation for focusing the mind during meditation, which awakens us to our oneness with reality and our divine, contented inner Self. This, fully illustrated in colour book, demonstrates how to use a wide range of Yoga Meditation practices as a portal to the higher consciousness. The book includes Paramhansa Yogananda's Kriya Yoga meditation techniques, making it an ideal practical handbook to Yogananda's *Autobiography of a Yogi*.

Yoga Meditation is now published in Italian, Spanish, French, Portuguese and Dutch.

Note: A new published edition of this book with a new design is now available. It is titled: ***Everyday Yoga Meditation***.

The Supreme Art and Science of Raja & Kriya Yoga – Stephen Sturgess, with foreword by David Frawley.

Singing Dragon, an imprint of Jessica Kingsley Publishers, London. **www.singingdragon.com**

The Supreme Art and Science of Raja and Kriya Yoga is a comprehensive and detailed master text on the subject of Raja and Kriya Yoga. The book authentically and accurately explains philosophical concepts and spiritual practices for the benefit of readers who are prepared to effectively use them. The book includes Paramhansa Yogananda's Kriya Yoga Meditation techniques and practices.

Mastering the Mind, Realising the Self – Stephen Sturgess.

O-Books, an imprint of John Hunt Publishing, London. **www.johnhuntpublishing.com**

Mastering the Mind, Realising the Self is an essential guide for an in-depth understanding of the mind and realising your true nature – God-Self.

The book includes Paramhansa Yogananda's Kriya Yoga Meditation techniques.

Kriya Yoga Resources

Authentic Kriya Yoga Meditation Teachers,
Organisations and Centres
Following the Teachings of Paramhansa Yogananda

London, UK

Stephen Sturgess, a devotee of Paramhansa Yogananda, and a direct disciple of Swami Kriyananda for 30 years, from whom he first received Kriya Initiation in 1983, was ordained in 2011 as a *Kriyacharya* (Kriya teacher) by Roy Eugene Davis (another direct disciple of Yogananda) to teach and initiate sincere truth seekers into Kriya Yoga Meditation. Stephen feels blessed to be of spiritual service to others in teaching Raja and Kriya Yoga. He teaches the Kriya meditation preparation techniques in London and gives *Kriya Initiation* only to those who are sincerely interested in Yogananda's teachings and awakening spiritually and have done the necessary spiritual training. Awakening to Self-knowing and Self-realisation is a gradual process and requires self-discipline and diligent practice with love, devotion, willingness, right attitude and perseverance.

Web: www.yogananda-kriyayoga.org.uk

Ananda Communities

Ananda Sangha (a worldwide organisation founded by Swami Kriyananda, a direct disciple of Paramhansa Yogananda), offers spiritual support and resources based on the teachings of Paramhansa Yogananda. There are Ananda spiritual communities in Nevada City, Sacramento, Palo Alto and Los Angeles, California; Seattle, Washington; Portland and Laurelwood, Oregon.
Web: www.ananda.org
www.expandinglight.org

Italy

Ananda Assisi (spiritual community and Kriya Yoga retreat)
Ananda Assisi, Via Montecchio, 61, 06025 Nocera Umbra (PG), Italy.
Web: www.ananda.it

India

Ananda India (spiritual communities at Gurgaon near New Delhi and Pune in North India)
Email: ananda@anandaindia.org
Web: wwww.anandaindia.org

Self-Realisation Fellowship

Paramhansa Yogananda founded the Self-Realisation Fellowship (SRF) in America in 1920 to make available the teachings of *Kriya Yoga* universally. The Self-Realisation fellowship (SRF) has its headquarters in Los Angeles, California. SRF has more than 500 temples and centres around the world and has members in 175 countries. In India and surrounding countries, Paramhansa Yogananda's work is known as Yogada Satsanga Society of India (YSS), which he founded in 1917.

The *SRF Lessons*, an in-depth home study course which provides Paramhansa Yogananda's step-by-step instructions in his Yoga methods including the *Kriya Yoga* science of meditation and his 'How-to-live' teachings, are available from the Self-Realisation Fellowship (SRF).

The SRF also has available for sale many books written by Paramhansa Yogananda, and a selection of DVD and CD talks and devotional music.

Address: Self-Realisation Fellowship, International Headquarters,
3880 San Rafael Avenue, Los Angeles, CA 90065-3219, USA.
Tel: (323) 225-2471
Web: www.yogananda-srf.org Self-Realisation Fellowship main website.
www.yssofindia.org (Yogoda Satsanga Society of India)

London Centre of Self Realisation Fellowship

London Centre of Self-Realisation, 82a Chiltern Street, London, W1U 5AQ.
Web: www.srf-london.org.uk

Centre for Spiritual Awareness

Ron Lindhan,
Centre for Spiritual Awareness, PO Box 7, Lakemont, Georgia, GA 30552-0001.

The Centre for Spiritual Awareness offers spiritual support and resources, seminars and Kriya meditation retreats based on the teachings of Paramhansa Yogananda.
Email: info@csa-davis.org or ron@csa-davis.org
Web: www.csa-davis.org

YouTube Videos of Paramhansa Yogananda's *Energisation Exercises*:

Paramhansa Yogananda's *Energisation Exercises*
1979 Recording of Swami Kriyananda teaching the *Energisation Exercises*

***Energisation Exercises* of Paramhansa Yogananda**
Led by Nayaswami Gyandev of Ananda School of Yoga and Meditation.

Paramhansa Yogananda *Energisation Exercises* Introduction New
The *Energisation Exercises*, as taught in the Ananda Course in Self-Realisation.

Autobiography of a Yogi:

Free online *Autobiography of a Yogi*
https://www.crystalclarity.com/yogananda/index.php

Nauli Kriya and Uddiyana Bandha:

Nauli Kriya Abdominal Massage Cleansing
http://pranayoga.co.in/asana/nauli-kriya-abdominal-massage-cleansing/
Uddiyana Bandha and Nauli
https://www.youtube.com/watch?v=l2R0dkzkbzE

Mala Beads for Meditation and *Japa* (repetition of a mantra)

Maha Mala is a small company based in New Delhi, India which specialises in making beautifully made health and wellness and meditation jewellery in the form of 108 bead necklaces, these necklaces can be used for *japa* (chanting with a mantra) or as jewellery. The term *Maha Mala* stems from two Sanskrit words; *Maha* meaning 'the great' and *Mala* meaning 'garland'.

Maha Mala started out as an idea to create sacred healing objects for use in personal rituals. This manifested into the stringing and restringing of *Malas* back in 2009. The *Malas* are designed by Nora Wendel and Piya Jain, the beautiful semi-precious stones and silver are hand sourced from Jaipur, Northern India for their quality and lustre. Each *mala* is hand strung using extra grade wire for durability and suppleness. Rudraksha, Tulsi and Sandalwood beads are also used in the making of their *mala* necklaces and bracelets.

Address: Matrika Creations Pvt. Ltd., 34 Aurobindo Place Market, Hauz Khas, New Delhi 110016.

Email: info@mahamala.com
Web: www.mahamala.com
Tel: +91 892-035-7711

CPSIA information can be obtained
at www.ICGtesting.com
Printed in the USA
BVHW032250270822
645705BV00008B/436

9 781788 789240